Community-Led Research

Community-Led Research

Walking New Pathways Together

Edited by Victoria Rawlings,
James L. Flexner and Lynette Riley

SYDNEY UNIVERSITY PRESS

First published by Sydney University Press
© Individual contributors 2021
© Sydney University Press 2021

Sydney University Press
Fisher Library F03
University of Sydney NSW 2006
Australia
sup.info@sydney.edu.au
sydneyuniversitypress.com.au

A catalogue record for this book is available from the National Library of Australia.

NATIONAL
LIBRARY
OF AUSTRALIA

ISBN 9781743327579 paperback
ISBN 9781743327586 epub
ISBN 9781743327647 mobi
ISBN 9781743327630 pdf

Cover artwork: detail from *Weavers* by Lynette Riley, 2010. The image used on the cover is taken from a kangaroo cloak (etching/poker work). It is inspired by a traditional story, provided by Kathy Marika, in a dance performance by Bangarra Dance Company (2010), in which people learnt the skills of weaving by studying spiders, and then created woven mats for sitting on and shelter. The woven mat is an ultimate example of the skills of weaving learnt by careful observation and working together; a well-wrought mat is a beautiful creation. This is also a symbol of what can happen when people work together productively, such as through community-led programs and research; they create a common and clear focus, they start with a small step and end up with something that can sustain and protect them for years. (Lynette Riley, 2021)

Cover design by Miguel Yamin.

Contents

v

Introduction: walking many paths towards a community-led paradigm

James L. Flexner, Victoria Rawlings and Lynette Riley

The idea that academic research needs to reach beyond the ivory tower has been around for a long time, gaining traction particularly after the 1960s as academics increasingly recognised that their research was neither politically neutral, nor only of interest to other academics. The concept of community as an important element of what we do has likewise become increasingly prominent across a variety of disciplines as a result of this impulse to reach beyond the walls of the university with our research. Somewhat ironically, in the 21st century environment of economic austerity and funding cuts, universities have returned to concepts of 'public impact' as they struggle to define their broader value in a rapidly changing political and social environment.

In this book, we introduce the concept of *community-led* as a critical new paradigm for academic research. We see Community-Led Research (CLR) as a distinctive, if related, approach to similar projects sometimes labelled Participatory Action Research (PAR; Kemmis & McTaggart, 2000; Kemmis, McTaggart & Nixon, 2014), or Community-Based Participatory Research (CBPR; Wilson, 2018).

J.L. Flexner, V. Rawlings & L. Riley (2021). Introduction: walking many paths towards a community-led paradigm. In V. Rawlings, J. Flexner & L. Riley (Eds.), *Community-Led Research: Walking new pathways together*. Sydney: Sydney University Press.

These types of research take the critical step towards attempting to make communities equal partners in the research process. As Wilson (2018, p. 1) notes:

> Distinguishing features of effective CBPR include: blurring the distinction between researchers and research participants, minimizing power imbalances, and researching in partnership with communities towards positive community outcomes that are sustainable beyond the life of the research.

CLR also shares an affinity with many kinds of 'activist' research that are pitched at different facets of broader projects concerned with 'social justice' (e.g. Atalay et al., eds., 2014; Ornstein, 2017; Smith & Wobst, 2005; Smith et al., 2019). In CLR the ways these kinds of approaches are defined and how they articulate with different projects will vary for a number of reasons, from the nature of the communities involved to the broader social and political landscapes in which they are located. The concept of social justice might work elegantly in certain CLR initiatives. Examples in this volume include Sampson, Katrack, Rawsthorne and Howard's approach to disaster planning and Rawlings and McDermott on self-harm among queer youth. In other cases, care must be taken when attempting to shoehorn Western concepts into community spaces in ways that might become culturally inappropriate. Flexner discusses in this volume the ways that local practices, beliefs and values are key to CLR in Vanuatu, where people might find the Western concept of social justice confusing or out of step with Melanesian traditions.

In this book, we aim to take steps beyond these models to establish a community-led approach to research. Rather than blurring the distinction between researchers and community, or minimising power imbalances, we seek to invert these dynamics as much as possible (Daniels-Mayes, this volume). What would the research environment be like if, rather than researchers coming up with ideas and then trying to work with communities to study them, the community was given the initiative to tell researchers what *they* want? What if the entire research process was then led from the community level, with the researcher placed in a position of facilitator, using their expertise not to direct but to serve community research interests?

We use the language of step-taking and movement intentionally here. In part this is because the reality of a CLR paradigm is largely unrealised. It is something we move towards, something we hope for and something we continue to work on, rather than something we have accomplished. We also use this language advisedly because of the significant Aboriginal and other Indigenous contributions to this volume, either through the identities of specific authors or more generally the close relationships in other authors' work with Indigenous communities. We find the metaphor of walking new pathways together inspiring as it invokes a journey together, with the end goal of communities serving as the guide, leading the way. Further, the concept of walking together implies something open-ended. We do not see this collection of essays as a final authoritative voice, but rather a beginning of a walk that should continue long into the future as we explore the ends of where a Community-Led approach to research can take us.

Community-Led Research: limitations and challenges

Frameworks such as PAR and CBPR signal a broad-based move away from the extractive and unequal relationships inherent to much academic research, especially research involving subaltern people. Far too often, university-based researchers, many with good intentions and robust ethical guidelines, have gone into different environments, gathered information, and turned that information into 'high-impact' publications (typically hidden behind insurmountable paywalls). The value of this work for the communities who have been 'researched' is unclear or non-existent. Certainly, many Indigenous peoples feel they have been 'studied to death', with no apparent benefit or even point to the work done to and at them. While it is tempting to assume such research is limited to the bad old days of colonialist research (for examples from anthropology, see Adams, 1987; Young, 2004), the reality is much academic research continues to work according to the extractive model, often in spite of the desires of the academics involved. Institutional emphasis on international rankings, productivity, and the continuous competition for research funding lead to an impossible situation for even the most well-meaning researchers.

Given the constant pressures on time and resources, work with communities often occurs on the sidelines of research, much of it done at the expense of other work bleeding into evenings and weekends as scholars put in extra hours to maintain the interpersonal relationships necessary to move towards a CLR approach. The authors in this volume are very aware of the limitations facing a true realisation of CLR in the contemporary academic sphere. These range from institutional, as with the funding structures that support research (Robinson et al., this volume), to structural, as with the ongoing legacies of colonial inequality (Flexner, this volume; Riley, this volume).

Besides the institutional problems on the academic side, there is also the question of community itself. It is tempting for outside researchers to imagine that communities represent coherent, cohesive, easily legible wholes: groups of similar people with similar ideals and desires (Frake, 2008). This is especially so when the researcher believes the community in question is small-scale or horizontally organised. In practice, of course, communities are the opposite: fractious, factional, and very difficult to understand without serious investment of time to develop close relationships with people. Indeed, the communities that are seen as horizontally organised can often be *more* complicated to work with, as decision-making processes are often dispersed, consensus-oriented, and above all time-consuming (Flexner, 2018).

Indeed, if there is one resource that will continue to challenge people walking the path towards CLR, it is *time*. A community-led paradigm asks us as researchers to take the time to reach out to people living beyond the bounds of academia (sometimes quite a long way outside, physically or otherwise); to initiate, grow and maintain close relationships; and to discuss, consider and continually re-evaluate our research approaches and outcomes. On the other side of the equation, collaborative research involves significant investment of time and resources from community members as well. One of the related challenges is how to recognise these efforts, through remuneration, co-authorship, or other means, while also making sure that the leadership role of involved community members is not compromised by things like payment (hence the need to frame CLR relationships in terms of reciprocity rather than dependency; Webster et al. this volume).

Thus, researchers interested in walking the path towards CLR find themselves in a bind. On one hand, our institutional positions and indeed access to resources to support research are contingent on our ability to appear productive to an output-oriented capitalist model of research (e.g. Cunningham and MacEachern, 2016, pp. 629–30; Scott, 2012, pp. 105–28). On the other hand, our ethical obligations push us towards an approach to research couched in terms of interpersonal relationships, sensitivity, and care (for the communities we work with, the environments we inhabit, the value of the knowledge we co-produce). As McMahon and McKnight (this volume) suggest, a move towards CLR is 'right, wrong, easy, and difficult', and yet for all the authors in this volume it is essential to advance research in this direction.

So, is it time for a rebellion? Many scholars are probing the limits and seeking alternatives to a system that extracts so much, both from research 'subjects' and the researchers themselves. Does CLR have natural allies, not only within the related fields of PAR and CBPR, but among scholars calling for a turn towards 'slow science' (Alleva, 2006; Stengers, 2011), or more broadly for a 'degrowth' approach to contemporary systems of production, including knowledge production (e.g. D'Alisa, Demaria & Kallis, 2015; Kallis, 2018)? Slow science asks researchers to take time to carefully consider their experiments, theories and results before rushing off to the next journal submission or grant application. It also discourages the idea, particularly among junior scholars, that our work as researchers is to be publication machines (and yes, we recognise the irony that this is yet another academic publication produced at a relatively fast pace, but we assure the readers it is a work of love, and dare we say, was actually *fun* or at least mostly enjoyable to work on).

Degrowth even more broadly recognises that the overall economic landscape in which we find ourselves is unsustainable, and basically undesirable on both environmental and human fronts (Krueger 2018; Wilkinson & Pickett 2009, 2018). If we want a habitable planet that is pleasant to live on (O'Neill et al., 2018), we need to reverse our current addiction to runaway growth, translated in the academic sphere as more publications, more grants, higher rankings, and above all, never-ending piles of work. At what point is it our role as researchers to say enough, to intentionally put the brakes on and slow the ever-accelerating pace of institutional productivity and pressure, to free up time, space and energy to go about the work of CLR properly?

From our perspective, we see these related projects as occurring in parallel with each other. Putting communities first in the work that we do will by necessity force us to slow down in many cases. We have to work at the pace that is comfortable for the people who are ideally leading the way in CLR. Further, this kind of research has the potential to bring about changes in the political ecology of research itself. Among other things, imagine the benefits across everything from carbon footprint to mental health if we could all occasionally shut off our laptops, smartphones and servers to invest time building community first, leading to research second, and then only carefully, slowly and intentionally. Rather than focusing on more and higher-impact outputs, CLR places the researcher as listener, learner, and sometimes facilitator, arranging access to particular areas of knowledge and expertise. It begins a walk down a path away from the capitalist model of constant productivity, and towards a space where research is about its quality, its value for real people, and its duty of care towards the world we all inhabit.

Walking many paths

This book does not offer a single overarching model for CLR. Rather, we approach this concept from a variety of backgrounds – cultural, disciplinary and personal. What ties these approaches together is the idea that community, understood broadly, has a critical role to play in the development of research over the remainder of the 21st century. The authors in this collection may have walked very different paths, but we arrive at the same place through our common interest in pushing the limits of the possible in our work with a variety of communities.

The book has a strong Australasian focus both in terms of geographical origin of the contributors and the locations of research sites. This book represents a particular, emplaced approach to CLR, including the voices of several scholars who are from the region's First Nations. It is not, however, parochial in outlook or approach. Rather, we provide a geographical emphasis that can offer a valuable comparative perspective for similar approaches in other parts of the world. Since this is an emerging field of research, it will be interesting to see how the form of CLR varies with geography, culture and history.

As the discussion above indicates, and many of the chapters that follow will suggest, we are still in the woods. As researchers interested in the CLR paradigm, we continue to walk on many small pathways of our own, sometimes parallel, sometimes overlapping, sometimes divergent. However, it is our hope in offering this volume that we begin moving towards the same direction, to a broader path that has more space for community members to walk with us, and indeed, to lead us in the directions they want to follow. For our readers, we hope this book encourages you to join us as we try to move towards clearer and brighter research landscapes in which community can be placed not just as equals, but as leaders in future research.

References

Adams, R. (1987). Homo Anthropologicus and Man-Tanna: Jean Guiart and the anthropological attempt to understand the Tannese. *Journal of Pacific History, 22*(1), pp. 3–14.

Alleva, L. (2006). Taking time to savour the rewards of slow science. *Nature, 443,* 271.

Cunningham, J. J. & MacEachern, S. (2016). Ethnoarchaeology as slow science. *World Archaeology, 48*(5), pp. 628–641. doi: 10.1080/00438243.2016.1260046

Atalay, S., Clauss, L. R., McGuire, Randall, H. & Welch, J. R. (Eds.). (2014). *Transforming archaeology: Activist practices and prospects.* New York: Routledge.

D'Alisa, G., Demaria, F. & Kallis, G. (Eds.). (2015). *Degrowth: A vocabulary for a new era.* New York: Routledge.

Flexner, J. L. (2018). Doing archaeology in non-state space. *Journal of Contemporary Archaeology, 5,* pp. 254–259.

Frake, C. O. (2008). Pleasant places, past times, and sheltered identity in rural East Anglia. In M. R. Dove & C. Carpenter (Eds.), *Environmental history: A historical reader,* pp. 435–456. Oxford: Blackwell.

Kallis, G. (2018). *Degrowth.* Newcastle upon Tyne: Agenda.

Kemmis, S. & McTaggart, R. (2000). Participatory action research. In N. K. Denzin & Y. S. Lincoln (Eds.), *Handbook of qualitative research,* Second ed., pp. 567–607. Thousand Oaks, CA: Sage.

Kemmis, S., McTaggart, R. & Nixon, R. (2014). *The action research planner.* Singapore: Springer.

Krueger, A. B. (2018). Inequality, too much of a good thing. In D. Grusky and S. Szelénya (Eds.). *The inequality reader: Contemporary and foundational readings in race, class and gender,* pp. 25–35. New York: Routledge.

O'Neill, D. W., Fanning, A. L., Lamb, W. F. & Steinberger, J. K. (2018). A good life for all within planetary boundaries. *Nature: Sustainability, 1,* pp. 88–95.

Ornstein, A. C. (2017). Social justice: History, purpose, and meaning. *Society, 54*(6), pp. 541–548.

Scott, J. C. (2012). *Two cheers for anarchism: Six easy pieces on autonomy, dignity, and meaningful work and play.* Princeton, NJ: Princeton University Press.

Smith, C. & Wobst, H. M. (2005). The next step: Archaeology for social justice. In C. Smith & H. M. Wobst (Eds.), *Indigenous archaeologies: Decolonizing theory and practice,* pp. 390–392. London: Routledge.

Smith, C., Burke, H., Gorman, A., Ralph, J., Pollard, K., Wilson, C. ... Jackson, G. (2019). Pursuing social justice through collaborative archaeologies in Aboriginal Australia. *Archaeologies, 15*(3), pp. 536–569.

Stengers, I. (2011). *Une autre science est possible! Manifeste pour un ralentissement des sciences.* Paris: La Découverte.

Wilkinson, R. & Pickett, K. (2009). *The spirit level: Why more equal societies almost always do better.* London: Penguin.

Wilkinson, R. & Pickett, K. (2018). *The inner level: How more equal societies reduce stress, restore sanity and improve everyone's wellbeing.* London: Penguin.

Wilson, E. (2018). Community-based participatory action research. In P. Liamputtong (Ed.). *Handbook of research methods in health social sciences,* pp. 1–15. Singapore: Springer.

Young, M. W. (2004). *Malinowski: Odyssey of an anthropologist, 1884–1920.* New Haven, CT: Yale University Press.

1

Community-Led Research through an Aboriginal lens

Lynette Riley

There is no argument that since the arrival of the British on the shores of what is now known as Australia, the First Nations people have been affected in ways that have at the least traumatised and irrevocably changed their lives, culturally, politically, legally and socially. It is also very clear that this is due to the impact of research undertaken by the British who focused, directed and in turn used this research in policy directions aimed at controlling Indigenous lives. This research commenced at the onset of contact, with the 'Secret Instructions' given to Cook on his journey to Australia:

> You are likewise to observe the Genius, temper, disposition and Number of the Natives, if there be any, and endeavour by all proper means to cultivate a Friendship and alliance with them, making them presents of such Trifles as they may Value, inviting them to Traffick, and Shewing them every kind of Civility and Regard: taking care however not to suffer yourself to be surprised by them, but to be always upon your guard against Accident.

L. Riley (2021). Community-Led Research through an Aboriginal lens. In V. Rawlings, J. Flexner & L. Riley (Eds.), *Community-Led Research: Walking new pathways together*. Sydney: Sydney University Press.

> You are also with the Consent of the Natives to take possession of the Convenient Situations in the Country in the Name of the King of Great Britain; or, if you find the Country uninhabited take possession for his Majesty by setting up Proper Marks and Inscriptions as first discovers and possessors. (See National Library of Australia, nd; Smith, 2010)

This research focus created the many ways in which Indigenous Australians have been viewed and then governed in Australia (Robinson, Flexner & Miller, this volume). Research was undertaken initially to find out about the people in the southern lands, so that the King of England and his people could best learn how to utilise them, their country and their resources for their own advantage. Engagement was viewed as a one-sided venture to benefit the British, not necessarily to create equitable relations or resources for Indigenous Australians. As such, it was in the interests of the British to claim Australia as being terra nullius, despite the writings of Cook in his journal that highlighted seeing Aboriginal people going about their daily lives and occupation of Australia from his ship. As Cowlishaw (2013) states, the emphasis in early research was to support Australia as being terra nullius, and was carried out without permission, consultation or involvement of First Nation peoples. Hart and Whatman (1998) observe that:

> The premise of most [Western] research and analysis has been locked into the belief that Indigenous Australians are anachronisms and, in defiance of the laws of evolution, remain a curiosity of nature, and are 'fair game' for research. The overt and covert presumptions underwriting all [Western] research and analysis into Indigenous Australian cultures is the inherent view of the superiority of Non-Indigenous society's cultures. (p. 3)

This chapter will provide an overview of the focus of research approaches and the impact of research on Indigenous Australia; what needs to be considered in research with Indigenous Australia; new debates and directions in research with Indigenous Australians through both international and national Indigenous influences, and why this is relevant; and what is often the reason Community-Led Research (CLR) is used in research. It will explore some of the do's, don'ts and concerns in where and why CLR should be used with Indigenous Australians.

Indigenous research impact

It must be recognised that until most recently the majority of research undertaken on Indigenous Australia has been through the lens and/or influenced by anthropological research, in both the framework of study – the methodologies used – and in the analysis of the data collected.

> The history of the literature on Aborigines is the history of anthropological hegemony and in the recent contributions from educationalists, historians, psychologists and political scientists, there is a tendency to rely on anthropologists' work for authoritative statements concerning Aboriginal traditions. It seems important therefore to define the limits of the anthropologist's area of expertise and admit that the discipline has no special authority in the area of what is called 'social change' or in the analysis of the kind of society into which Aborigines have been incorporated. The bulk of social anthropology in Australia on Aboriginal society until recently may be more accurately described as social archaeology. (Cowlishaw, 2013, p. 75)

Cowlishaw (2013) in her review of the work of anthropologists and their research of Indigenous Australians, stated that anthropologists have been extremely influential in how Aboriginal people and their societies were viewed and 'understood by Australian intellectuals, politicians, journalists and now by the land courts' (p. 61). What is important to clarify here is that whilst this research was done on Aboriginal people, the influence of the research in controlling Aboriginal lives, through the development of policies and ongoing structural systems and practices, is the key to the ongoing marginalisation of Indigenous peoples (Moore, Pybus, Rolls & Moltow, 2017).

Figure 1.1, showing the Indigenous research impact flowchart, highlights the impact of research on First Nations peoples and

INDIGENOUS RESEARCH

Government
Policies &
Practices
——————
——————
Systems &
Structures

Indigenous
Studies

Community
Engagement

Non-Indigenous
Knowledge

TEACHINGS – LEARNINGS

Pedagogy

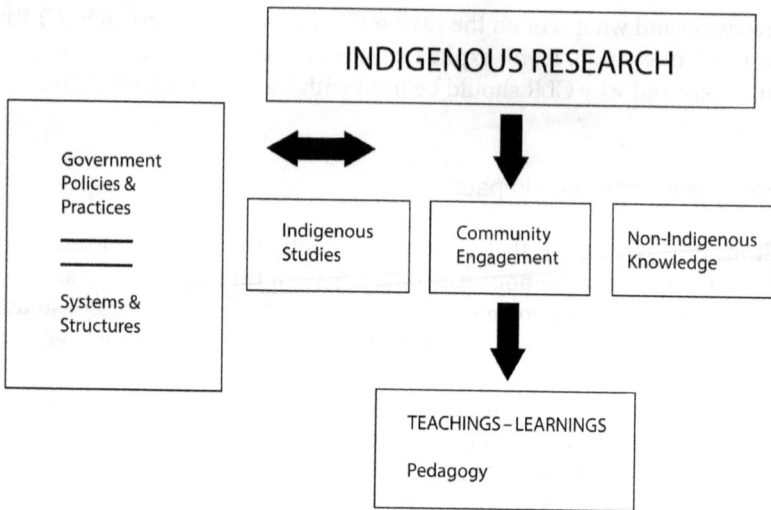

Figure 1.1 Indigenous Research Impact

how it has governed the studies undertaken, the approaches to Indigenous community engagement, and specifically the knowledge and understanding of non-Indigenous Australians:

Research undertaken has created and affected:

1. Indigenous studies: the type of studies done in relation to Indigenous people, initially undertaken and developed to work in remote communities with Indigenous peoples;
2. Indigenous community engagement: the style and type of Indigenous community engagement, often using a patriarchal and Western-dominated approach; and
3. Non-Indigenous people's knowledge of Indigenous Australians, which helped govern personal and wider relationships in society; and one could also say led to the rise of racism and the stereotypes attributed to Indigenous peoples in Australia.

These three factors have been influential in forming government policies and the practices of organisations and structures for not only social systems in Australia, such as education, health, housing and employment opportunities, but also for how private organisations and businesses have interacted with Indigenous Australians. This has in turn influenced teachings and learning about Indigenous Australia. The pedagogical approaches in education with Indigenous students – that is, the ways in which Indigenous people have been taught, or been allowed to engage in education – and the ways in which learning through curriculum developed for all other Australians, outside of anthropology, about First Nations peoples have been undertaken in the past and currently are seen as relevant or irrelevant, across all levels of education (Moore, Pybus, Rolls & Moltow, 2017; Cowlishaw, 2013).

The influence of these processes combines to impact the range of policies and practices utilised in Australia, which form our social systems and the structures to govern our nation. This in turn affects Indigenous peoples' place in Australian society – how they are viewed and the ways in which they have been affected by past and ongoing policies and practices, which has in effect led to exclusion on multiple levels in our current society (World Health Organization, 2019; Popay, et al., 2008). This therefore means that to ignore the past research undertaken on Indigenous Australians, how this research was undertaken, and the Western methodologies and influence in analysing this data, would mean maintaining a coloniser's view of Australia and ensuring Indigenous Australians remain marginalised. It is imperative therefore that we make sure that Indigenous Australians are able to determine what research is required to be undertaken and how this will be done in order to ensure their cultural, political and social needs are met, and are not simply determined by external agencies.

History of research approaches on Indigenous Australia

Cowlishaw (2013) has described six layers of research through anthropology that have influenced political and social structures for Indigenous Australians since contact commenced with the British in Australia in 1788 – the first two being the Moving Frontiers (1800s–1930s) and the Protection Era (c. 1860s–1890s). Cowlishaw (2013) comments that these two eras are reflective of maintaining the premise and legal doctrine of Australia being founded on 'terra nullius'. That is, that no people lived in Australia, it was not populated and had no productive civilisation occupying the lands. This doctrine has been refuted by many people since this time (Pascoe, 2018). The research in these two eras, whilst focused on 'terra nullius', also reinforced this premise and was undertaken on Indigenous Australians without their permission, consultation or involvement. Cowlishaw (2013) states that a clear issue was the way in which Indigenous people were viewed in this research, in that:

> Anthropologists' definition of Aborigines was always dependent on notions of their cultural integrity and homogeneity. No concepts or theories were developed within Australian anthropology which could adequately deal with either relations between the indigenous population and the invaders or with changes in either. (p. 61)

and that further:

> when anthropologists did conduct research with non-traditional groups the very vocabulary of 'caste' and 'blood' with which such groups were described, relied on biological ideas of race, and the search for the traditional also relies in the final analysis on the reification of race. (p. 61)

Clearly, anthropology was used to support the Western belief of one theory of evolution – and the idea of Westerners' own superiority, seeing themselves at the top of the evolutionary ladder, was well entrenched in research.

The third era discussed by Cowlishaw (2013) is Coercive Segregation (the late 1890s into the 20th century) which was based on a conservative approach that determined the importance of having national development; that is, one national identity into which all other cultures and races must be subsumed – a 'White Australia' identity. This in turn diminished Indigenous culture, languages and narratives in their landscapes, placing Indigenous peoples at the bottom of the social hierarchy through social marginalisation due to their cultural differences.

The fourth era of research reinforced a need for Assimilation (1930s –1960s; Cowlishaw, 2013), and created a revisionist reinterpretation. This led to some correction of the conservative approach and allowed Indigenous voices to be heard and some aspects of hidden or excluded histories to come to light; however, the key focus was on forcing First Nations peoples to divest themselves of their culture and take on the cultural mores of the British.

The fifth era in research introduced Rights and Self-Determination (1970s–2000; Cowlishaw, 2013) and opened greater dialogue, engagement and participation for Indigenous people. This was often due to Indigenous people gaining political voices and being heard on a national and international level, with their fights for Indigenous rights. The sixth era of research, Indigenous Directives, arose since the 2000s, and has created more forums where Indigenous peoples can direct and inform what Indigenous Studies should be and has also generated new research paradigms.

As such, we can clearly see a change in the approaches being undertaken in research concerning Indigenous peoples, as reflected in Figure 1.2.

Driese and Mazurski (2018), in Figure 1.2, highlight that where research is undertaken *about* Indigenous people it is unilateral and allows no engagement with Indigenous people and all the control of the research is outside of Indigenous peoples' parameters. Research *with* Indigenous people allows some negotiation, but control of the research – who runs it, where it is undertaken and who is involved – again is outside of Indigenous control. Research *by* Indigenous people allows for an empowered situation to occur, where Indigenous people control what research they want undertaken, who is involved in the research, where the research occurs and how the data gets analysed. When carrying out research we need to be very clear how the research is undertaken to allow optimum empowerment of Indigenous communities, to resolve their own community directions and crises and provide self-determination for them and their communities.

What do we mean by this?

By
research
by
Aboriginal
people

[empowered]

With
research
with
Aboriginal
people

[negotiated]

About
research
about
Aboriginal
people

[unilateral]

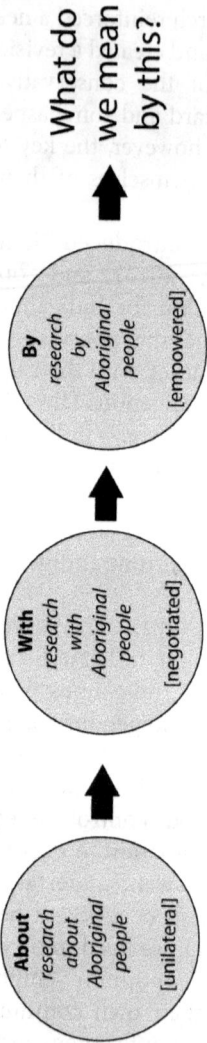

Figure 1.2 Research and Aboriginal People (after Driese & Mazurski, 2018, p. 14)

What do we need to consider to empower Indigenous research?

In assessing what is required to empower Indigenous peoples through research, the responses to the following questions need to be known, considered and understood.

1. Indigenous research methodologies – how do they differ from other areas of research?
   Be aware of what is entailed in Indigenous research methodologies, how these may differ from or support Western research methodologies, and how they empower Indigenous peoples' directions.
2. What does privileging voices in research mean? How does this influence knowledge and teaching?
   Acknowledge and learn how research often privileges Western voices and rhetoric and how we can change the way we undertake research to privilege Indigenous voices and empower Indigenous communities.
3. Are Indigenous research methodologies important? Why?
   Study the impact of research that has a Western approach and that may not privilege Indigenous voices, and how this may have a negative impact on Indigenous communities' needs and goals. Alternatively, how can this be changed to ensure Indigenous voices are privileged to ensure positive impacts for Indigenous peoples?
4. What does disrupting Western research mean?
   Explore the differences between Western and Indigenous research methodologies and what must be done to empower Indigenous communities through their research requirements.
5. What does working with Indigenous communities mean?
   Assess the importance of different cultural protocols and how these influence community engagement and voice in research practice and procedures.
6. How can we ensure Indigenous voices are included?
   Ensure research methodologies commence with Indigenous voices and Indigenous control of the research processes, directions, analysis and outcomes.
7. Why is 'decolonality' important? What does it mean in research and in the transmission of knowledge?

Decolonality starts with assessing the self in understanding the purpose of the research to be carried out and who the research serves to support. If in this reflective process you realise that the research does not support the research participants of the research – that is, the real value of the research goes towards empowering the researcher – then you must check the validity of the research and acknowledge whose privilege it serves. Decolonality starts with self-reflection and understanding the ultimate purpose of the research.

8. What is the impact of Indigenous histories and representation through museums? Understand the role museums have played in collecting and cataloguing Indigenous peoples and their cultures. Issues that need to be raised are:

(i) What consultative processes have been used and what processes have been put into place to allow Indigenous communities to veto particularly significant cultural items from public display?

(ii) Historiography: The need to understand actions in the past from the viewpoint of the participants – scientist, missionary, Aboriginal Elder, etc. – and how each must be understood in light of the era's political and social barriers.

(iii) Museums are sites for continued learning in that they have acquired many cultural items, which may now need greater cultural and social commentary from Indigenous peoples; and/or greater access to view items in privacy to allow communities to mourn the loss of items and remember people these items were linked to; and/or have items of significance returned, through repatriation programs.

(iv) Determine what steps you would take in a museum when working with human remains; consider different cultural protocols if the human remains are Aboriginal, Islander or European.

9. What impact does nationhood, statehood and sovereignty have on us as Australians?

Remember that different policies reflect the directions of each nation. This will have an impact on how policies are implemented and the level and type of engagement of people from different Indigenous cultural backgrounds.

10. What is important about Indigenous cultural and intellectual property and how does it impact on Indigenous research methodologies?
The understanding of who has the final say regarding the ownership of cultural items and the provision of intellectual property is the practice of privileging Indigenous peoples' authority to veto and/or support research, items collected and/or displayed.

11. What is the importance of place-, space- and time-based methodologies? What role does perspective play in these?
Byrne and Nugent (2004) discuss this within the following three parameters of knowledge keeping and re-telling, which requires a clear understanding of the use and influence of:
(i) Archives – who collects them, where they are kept, access to records, style of recording keeping, recognition of oral heritage through yarning, and styles and types of mapping. The issues are: what exists, what are the gaps, who interprets this material, and the impact of change across different eras.
(ii) Landscape – mapping spatial areas, what or who influences changes in landscapes, what lies beneath the layers of history and keeping of records, what are Aboriginal interpretations of landscapes vs Western interpretations? The issues are: what's in a name, history of contact, policies and wider community engagement or exclusion for Indigenous peoples, places of control, and are Indigenous people and their places of significance used as tourist attractions in differing landscapes.
(iii) Lives – through lived stories and histories; are they published or oral stories and histories, what is used as corroborating evidence, what is visible and invisible in these histories, recognising how cultural lives are not included in archives. The issues are: the interpretation of these histories – who does it, the quality of past recordings of people's stories, the ethics employed in the collection of material, and is there understanding and recognition of intellectual property in the collection and use of material.

Sommerville (2013, p. 42), in discussing her research and the importance of Aboriginal peoples' perspectives of place, space and time, reflects that inclusion of and listening to Aboriginal people provided her with an important story that might offer a way to enter a different sort of understanding of place and identity in Australia …

I had many unanswered questions. Where did this story fit into the landscape? What were the places of its beginning and ending? How did it connect with the multitudes of other stories about the creation of the landscape and all of its creatures? These are complex questions that are part of a larger context that has taken me ten years to begin to unravel … So I go to a place I have been to before, a taken-for-granted beach place, like all other beach places in Australia. On the one hand, I have a deep sense of the significance of this place, the intensity of the storylines that intersect there, but on the other hand, it is just a normal beach place with a caravan park and estuary, headlands, beach, and sea. How do I reconcile these things? What sense can I make of the intersection of these meanings? In a sense these questions are the quintessential questions about writing.

Indigenous histories, culture, stories and perspectives intersect to create a depth of knowledge about the Australian landscape for different places, spaces and times; if these are not included, there is no real understanding of Australia.

Processes for Indigenous research

It is vital that researchers (Robinson, Flexner & Miller, this volume) understand the different cultural protocols (Welsh & Burgess, this volume) required in any research process and that these will be different to the requirements of Western research processes. The model of the processes used in the Kinship Online Project (Mooney, Riley & Howard-Wagner, 2016) differs from Western research processes.

The following articulates the various stages and actions undertaken in the research model established by Mooney, Riley & Howard-Wagner (2016, pp. 24–27). This model demonstrates how research with Indigenous people (Webster, Hill, Hall & See, this volume; Welsh & Burgess, this volume) needs to be more critical and reflective through the provision of longer time frames, to guarantee appropriate research is undertaken with the consent of Aboriginal people and for the benefit of their communities. It is important to point out that in this model the key to the different engagement processes is that for Aboriginal people it is the validity of the people involved through relationships and knowing one another, through following Aboriginal protocols, that will be the primary focus of who should be engaged – from both the academic and the Aboriginal community – in the research. In the Western processes, the engagement in research is based on the credentials of the researcher, such as having a doctorate, which is acknowledged and recognised through Western academia.

The stages for Aboriginal engagement identified in this model were:

Precursor – Informal

This informal process commenced at least six to twelve months prior to any research ideas in order to gauge people's thoughts on whether they believed it was a worthy project. Through meeting with local community, engaging with potential research assistants and assessing venues and locations for meetings, it was ensured that the Aboriginal community protocols for the validation of researchers were adhered to.

Stage 1: What if?

Ask questions and work with the community to determine the viability of the research. Some questions asked were: What if we were to submit a proposal for a grant to do ...?; Would you think this is a good idea?; Would you be supportive of the research?; In what way could you be supportive?; Where could we hold workshops?; Who do you think could/should be involved in organising events/components for this research in ...?; Who should be invited to participate in the workshops for the research?; If we apply for the grant, and if and when the ethics process is cleared, does anyone want to be contacted further about the research?

This undertaking first required speaking informally to various Aboriginal agencies in the community and members of the local Aboriginal community and wider region – to see who thinks the research is worthy and who would want to be involved. Additionally, statewide or regional consultation may also be required if the research falls under the parameters of any regional or statewide organisation.

Stage 2: Informal and formal notification

Local Aboriginal community organisers were recognised as valid and were needed to be seen as neutral within the Aboriginal community; able to speak across and for a wide cross-section of the community; and have reliable access to resources to assist in the research project.

Stage 2 occurred following the university's formal notification of the grant and ethics approval and prior to the research being conducted. This also involved building research relationships and providing a research training session for community members, looking at issues such as: what research ethics processes are, how and why the research is being run, the importance of the community being involved and their role in the project. This helped create a formalised plan while being mindful to build the local community's capacities in what formal research is and ensuring additional time for discussions to understand academic research and the ethics processes involved. This meant that people in the community gained a more in-depth knowledge of academic research, which they could use should any research proposals be put to their community in the future.

Stage 3: Familiarisation with ethical research processes

Familiarise the Aboriginal community with the academic ethics process and how this influenced the collection of the research data. The following steps were undertaken:

i. Interviewing process: Ethics process. A workshop was held for the Aboriginal community to provide an oral explanation and an information sheet on university ethics processes, aligned with their involvement to ascertain their expectations of and objectives for the research. This meant all stakeholders had a clear understanding of their roles and who they could go to if any problems arose during the research.

ii. Interviewing process: Data collection. A workshop was held to discuss the data collection process with local community research assistants. These discussions covered issues such as: ethics, identifying participants for interviews, the type of information sought, and the types of questions we could ask participants.

Stage 4: Formalising the process with the local community

i. Finalising the research: Formal and informal. Continuous phone and email contact be seen as keeping the process on track, but must not be seen as harassing participants; it is imperative for ongoing relationships, that face-to-face follow-up visits from the academic team be made regularly in the interview process and research completion; and in turn include participants in the evaluation and how the reports will be written, such as, what the language style will be, for example, Plain English.

ii. Follow-up: Formal and informal. Hold a survey of the community interviewers who accumulated the data and collect their perspectives on the strengths and problems with the research process.

iii. Dissemination: Formal and informal. Determine with the community how the research results should be disseminated, debrief how they thought the project went, and gather ideas for improvements. Always ensure provision of a verbal report, which will also include a demonstration of material collected, followed by the written report.

iv. Production of the final report. Produce a final report detailing the research: aims, approach, methodology; and the impact and evaluation of the project. Include community input from surveys and/ or oral comments from community feedback sessions.

Western research – Aboriginal community engagement

As stated by Mooney, Riley and Howard-Wagner (2016, p. 27), a key concern in any Western research which aims to have strong community engagement is:

> When carrying out research with Aboriginal people and in Aboriginal communities, there is often tension between Western approaches – how the university and ethics tell you it must be

done and how Aboriginal people view the research being carried out. The role of the researchers, both Indigenous and non-Indigenous, is to ensure that while the ethical processes are adhered to, Aboriginal people and their communities feel engaged and know that the researchers aren't in control of them. Hence it is vital that researchers understand how to conduct research with Aboriginal people and their communities. If researchers are not culturally competent, it may mean that Aboriginal communities have a 'bad' experience or could be 'harmed in some way' (see Sherwood, 2010, cited in Mooney, Riley & Howard-Wagner, 2016) and not wish to be engaged in future research projects, thus creating difficulties into the future.

Therefore, it is imperative to be clear on what we mean by community participation in research and how this influences academics in the use of community-led approaches in research, to ensure Indigenous voices and directions for research are privileged.

Debates and directions

Debates surrounding Indigenous peoples' level of engagement in research and their rights in research have been substantial. Early declarations of support for Indigenous people have been published by a range of organisations, most particularly in relation to work with linguistics and the research undertaken on Indigenous languages, such as that released by the Australian Linguistic Society (1982, n.p.), which stated that:

In any dealings between a community and linguists, the community has the following rights:
1. To finalize clear and firm negotiations to the community's satisfaction before the linguistic fieldwork is undertaken.
2. To know and understand what their work involves, their obligations to the community and the restrictions they must observe using a paid local interpreter at all times if the community so requests.

3. To request a trial period before giving full permission for the research to continue.

4. To control research if the community wishes and also to request the linguist to consult with relevant community organizations where appropriate.

5. To ask for their help in language matters, training and other ways.

6. To receive regular summaries and results of the linguist's work written and presented in a way that the community can understand.

7. To privacy and secrecy with respect to person's names, confidential information, secret/sacred material and publication.

8. To approve the content of material before publication.

9. To see its members adequately paid in cash or otherwise for their services, and properly acknowledged in publications.

10. To negotiate for a share of royalties from any publications.

11. To be advised and receive a copy of any subsequent publications related to the research.

From these basic tenets, which are concerned with negotiated participation, other agencies have published their support of these rights, such as: Federation of Aboriginal and Torres Strait Islander Languages (2004); NSW Board of Studies (2008); Australian Institute of Aboriginal and Torres Strait Islander Studies (2012); and National Health and Medical Research Council (2018; 2003). The key concern is to what extent have these guidelines been understood in research, adhered to and actioned? If these current guidelines were to be followed by all researchers or agencies working with Indigenous communities, community-led approaches would be seen as central and an imperative in all research that might be considered, planned or undertaken.

Within these tenets are the ways in which Indigenous knowledge is given authority and authenticity, as often Western processes within systems such as universities are often valued more highly than Indigenous peoples' knowledge systems and ways of doing business (Moore, Pybus, Rolls & Moltow, 2017). In such cases we need to assess the research sources and ask what is seen as being provided with more priority and/or authority and what is seen as more authentic, such as:

Elders or archives?

- What source is given more prominence or validity?

Language recording and revival – speakers or linguists?

- Who is considered a valued speaker and by whom?

Expert rhetoric

- Who is considered an expert in research and by whom?

Discourses of death and sleep – where often non-Indigenous sources proclaim that there is no knowledge or it is 'dead', yet for Indigenous people it is seen as 'hidden' or asleep' and just waiting to be re-woken. Who has the cultural knowledge and expertise?

- Often Indigenous people may be hesitant to volunteer their cultural knowledge, due to past historical negative policies and punishment for this knowledge. As such, who has knowledge and who is willing to provide this can change, as Indigenous people feel more valued and respected and have developed a relationship of trust with researchers.

Language 'engineering'

- Whose language is being used to record material and how material is translated to ensure it reflects Indigenous peoples' knowledge and it isn't being 'Westernised'.

Protocols, power and control

- The benefits of gatekeeping and/or who are the gatekeepers and why is this control used?

Sources, veracity and usefulness of the material collected

- Who gets to ascertain this? Westerners or Indigenous people who have direct kinship relationships to the area and knowledge?

Access

- Who can speak, learn and teach the material being given and researched?

Collaboration or competition?

- Is there a clear understanding of who has the right to veto or acquiesce to the material collected?

Collective responsibility

- Is there a clear agreement on a collective responsibility for who has the rights to be the person who has the cultural knowledge and where does this come from?

These issues listed above need to be openly challenged and debated to ensure Indigenous voices are privileged in research undertaken.

A key question we need to ask as researchers, particularly in our roles within universities, is: How do we, as Aboriginal and non-Aboriginal researchers, undertake Indigenous or Indigenous-focused research and meet the requirements of the university and Aboriginal communities?

This is particularly important as we need to understand, within the university context, the overall purpose of research we are asked to undertake. In answering this question, we need to explore what methodologies we are using, whose voice it privileges, and how can we ensure Indigenous peoples are able to lead the research?

Methodologies

Is assessing these issue raised above, we need to be aware of the range of Indigenous academics who are challenging and utilising Indigenous methodologies in research (Moore, Pybus, Rolls & Moltow, 2017). Below are some Indigenous researchers and methodologies demonstrating research methodologies incorporating Indigenous ways or knowing, being and doing.

Internationally – First Nations academics in Canada, USA, Aotearoa (New Zealand). Nationally – Indigenous academics in Australia who have been influencing methodological reform. These lists are preliminary lists and not limited to these Indigenous academics. Take the time to look at the work being done by these influencers, and ask how they might shape your own work as an academic.

International Indigenous influencers

Bryan Brayboy	Critical Tribal Race Theory & Learning on Country
Linda Tuhiwai Smith	Decolonising Research & Culturally Appropriate Research
Graham Smith	Maori Theorising & Indigenising Education
Fiona Cram	Constructive Conversations
Jo-ann Archibald	Story Work
Margaret Kovach	Relational Research
Suzanne SooHoo	Culturally Responsive Research Methodologies
Mere Berryman	Culturally Responsive Research Methodologies
Anne Nevin	Culturally Responsive Research Methodologies
Shawn Wilson	Research is Ceremony & Building Knowledges for Community
Gregory Cajete	Ethobotany – Culturally Based Science/Indigenous Perspectives in Science

Australian Indigenous influencers

Martin Nakata	Indigenous Standpoint Theory
Aileen Moreton-Robinson	Indigenous Women's Standpoint Theory
Tyson Yunkaporta	8 Ways & Protocols in Working with Community
Nerida Blair	Lilyology
Karen Martin	Booran Mirraboopa – Ways of Knowing, Being & Doing
Bronwyn Fredericks	Indigenous Engagement in Research
Lester-Irabinna Rigney	Reforming Indigenous Research – defined and controlled by Aboriginal people
Dawn Bessarab	Yarning

Australian Indigenous influencers	
Miriam-Rose Ungunmerr-Baumann	Deep Listening
Mark Rose	Practitioners Blindspot & Reflection
Wendy Baarda	Cultural Difference

To understand and utilise community-led approaches requires being aware of how to best use and acknowledge Indigenous people's methodological approaches.

What's working?

In working with Indigenous peoples it is important to understand what methodological approach is working and which communities it works in, as not all approaches will work with all Indigenous communities for a range of reasons, such as:

- History of contact and interrelationships developed in the community between Indigenous and non-Indigenous people – this is linked closely to experiences of racism in the community.
- Academic levels of education of Indigenous people in communities and their previous experiences – positive and negative – in education.
- Social levels – health, economic position, that is, poverty level, availability of work in the community, and housing access; these factors are all tied into one another and will influence Indigenous peoples' engagement with academics.

As an academic, being aware of and understanding these influences for Indigenous peoples assists in determining the best approaches that work for different Indigenous communities (see Welsh & Burgess this volume).

Influences on Indigenous research and purposes of the research?

It is essential when developing research approaches and engagement with Indigenous peoples that there is an understanding of what Indigenous peoples expect to gain from the research (Webster, Hill, Hall & See, this volume), such as that elucidated by Rigney (2003, p. 39):

- Resistance as the emancipatory imperative in Indigenist research
- The political integrity of Indigenist research
- Privileging Indigenous voices in Indigenist research:

Rigney (2003) is highlighting first, that Indigenous people are often resistant to research that does not benefit them and that this is often proved to them by their many past experiences of being researched, with no benefit to them or their communities. This establishes their right to refuse any research and it is in their interests to do so – without prior and informed information and proof of how the research will benefit them and their communities. Second, that research has often been tied to political agendas of control and disempowerment, taking Indigenous people's resources and excluding them from mainstream processes – enforcing them as marginal citizens within their nation states. Third, that research must ensure Indigenous voices are privileged and are seen as the first voice in determining what research needs to be undertaken, how it will be undertaken, how the data will be analysed and by whom, and how the data will be written and distributed. It is only when these three research issues are openly addressed and resolved that Indigenous people should enter into any research proposal.

Indigenous research teaching and learning

What academics should be aiming to achieve in their research for Indigenous peoples is to:

- Build knowledge of pre-contact culture, colonial violence and intergenerational legacies.
- De-mythicise pre-contact culture.

- Equip academics to practise in more culturally sensitive, appropriate and safe ways for Indigenous people.
- Reduce ethnocentric and class biases, and accommodate differing social and cultural backgrounds.
- Change past representations of Aboriginality, based on stereotyping, racialised narratives and negative representations that sought to inferiorise Indigenous peoples and their cultures.
- Contribute to a society inclusive of Aboriginal and Torres Strait Islander peoples as equal citizens, without the requirement to abandon their cultural heritage.

These aims should be clearly articulated in all research proposals in relation to Indigenous peoples.

Communication, consultation and interaction

The key to research and outcomes which lead to sustainable change for communities is the level of communication, consultation and communication that exists (Welsh & Burgess, this volume), aligned with knowledge of each other, such as for service delivery agencies, knowledge of Indigenous peoples' culture, cultural operations and protocols; and for Indigenous people, it is knowledge of the service delivery agency's operations, systems, processes and strategies for achieving aims, goals and practice. If these do not coincide, or are one-sided, then sustainability will not be created. Figure 1.3 outlines the interaction between communities and service delivery agencies for sustainable practices to occur through communication, consultation and interaction.

Community – understanding of institutional processes

Institution – understanding of Indigenous history, culture and interrelations

Figure 1.3 presents the interaction of the community – on the horizontal line – who may have a low or high understanding of service delivery agencies. The vertical line represents the service delivery agencies' understanding and knowledge of Indigenous communities, cultures and histories, which is either low or high. The intersection of

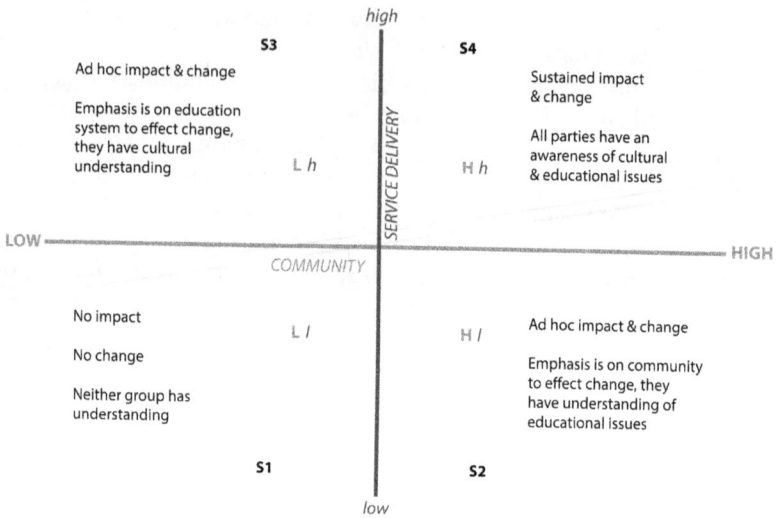

Figure 1.3 Communication, Consultation and Interaction (Riley-Mundine, 2007).

these will create either no change, ad hoc change or sustainable and ongoing changes, as outlined below:

Scenario 1 (S1): Indicates that neither the Indigenous community nor the service delivery agency have any knowledge of one another. This means that there is no communication between the groups and that no change will occur to operations for the community. It may also indicate that active racism is occuring in this community, which will impact on the interactions between parties.

Senario 2 (S2): Indicates that the community has knowledge and understanding of the organisation, but that the agency have little to no understandng of the community. In such a scenario, much of the work for change is coming from the community and this is a one-sided effort. This may lead to ad hoc change; but this may cease when community members cannot sustain the effort.

Scenario 3 (S3): Is where the agency is leading the change process. This may indicate the effort is again one-sided and may be placed on the shoulders of a small number of individuals, who have knowledge of the community's histories and cultural processes; but that the community have no knowledge of the organisation. This will produce ad hoc change whilst the service delivery personnel are engaged; but when they leave, the change may not continue and is not sustained.

Scenario 4 (S4): This is the optimum scenario and indicates that the community and service delivery agency are fully aware of one another, are engaged and have open and regular communication. This will lead to growth and sustainable change for all parties.

A question to ask in any proposed research is which of these scenarios applies to the academic, the Indigenous communities and the organisations they are working through? Understanding where agencies and Indigenous communities fit in these scenarios enables strategies to be built so that ongoing work leads to positive and sustainable practice.

Community-Led Research – when should it be done?

A key issue in relation to determining when and how community-led approaches and research should be undertaken revolves around when is CLR considered important or necessary? Often community-led options are as a result of ongoing crises in the community (see Sampson, Katrak, Rawsthorne & Howard, this volume) and the government 'giving up' trying to restore order or control the community situation. They then make contact with key community members and offer to allow them to take control, that is, take on board a community-led approach (Kar & Chambers, 2008; see McMahon & McKnight this volume; Sampson, Katrak, Rawsthorne & Howard, this volume). In this scenario, the ideology behind CLR is that the authority feels they have nothing to lose and they will let Indigenous peoples have a go. An example in education is a project undertaken at Cherbourg Primary School – a primarily Aboriginal school, located on an old Aboriginal Reserve in Queensland. In this case, an Indigenous teacher, Chris Sarra (2012), was given the position at the school as the principal, as the alternative was to close the school, due to the high failure rates and non-attendance of the students.

Chris Sarra turned the school around by incorporating strong educational expectations and Aboriginal protocols. The key issue here was that Chris Sarra did not use strategies that had not been discussed, written about or petitioned for, before this incident. These strategies were simply made possible when the authorities gave up and allowed the school to become community-led.

CLR has been proven to work, but depends on the combination of two key strategies:

(i) Attitudes and behaviours of facilitators – where what is required is a 'combination of boldness, empathy, humour and fun ... to enable people to confront their unpalatable realities' (Kar & Chambers, 2008, p. 9); and

(ii) Sensitive support of institutions – where there is 'consistent flexible support' (Kar & Chambers, 2008, p. 9), not an ad hoc program (as highlighted in Figure 1.3) or test-like approaches, which change dependent on the particular mindset of the institution's personnel and who are in control at any given time.

When these two strategies combine, we see sustainable practice occurring with sound achievable outcomes. As academics we need to be very clear about our role in CLR. Be aware of the purpose of the research and where the research will leave the community.

A table entitled 'Basics: The Key Attitudes and Behaviours in Community-Led Research', created by Kar and Chambers (2008, pp. 10–11) in their community-led projects for improving sanitation in Indian communities, provides a clear list of ways academics should and shouldn't interact with community members they are seeking to engage with in community-led approaches for projects.

These are essential steps in creating open and ongoing communication with community groups for research and projects.

Kar and Chambers (2008) go on to discuss the sequence of steps required in ensuring a community-led approach drives research and projects. These are:

Pre-triggering: what establishes the need for any research or project to be created?

- Community selection: is this based on ongoing community crises and needs to solve or resolve a local community issue?
- Introductions and building rapport: who instigates the research or project; ensure appropriate cultural protocols are adhered to; and that interrelationships and rapport are built before any plans are created.

Triggering: who are the stakeholders involved, and what roles will be required of them for the research/project?

- Participatory profile analysis: who needs to be involved in the research/project; build a profile of stakeholders and what their role may be in the research/project.
- Ignition moment: what instigates the moment the research/project must commence and who are the stakeholders in this process?

Post-triggering: how will the research/project be carried out with clearly articulated benefits for the community?

- Action planning by the community: ensure that community stakeholders have a privileged and controlling voice in the planning of the research: what it entails, how it will be carried out, and who the key stakeholders will be. Ensure that the time frame of the work to be undertaken and when is clearly articulated, so that all stakeholders understand their roles.

Scaling up and going beyond the project: when the research or project is completed, what are future plans?

- Determine a future beyond the immediate research/project to ensure ongoing sustainability of the research/project outcomes and relationships.

Planning is the key to all research and projects; the key issue in community-led is the significance given to the stakeholders involved at the community level and the manner in which they are privileged and have control of research and projects.

Conclusion

This chapter has sought to provide an overview of who has been influential in research approaches and the impact of that research on Indigenous Australians; how research has often viewed Indigenous Australians as subjects or excluded them from how research is planned, carried out and analysed. In recognising research approaches undertaken we must acknowledge and use Indigenous protocols, ethics and methodologies of research collection to ensure Indigenous voices are privileged; and as academics we must be clear about what CLR entails, to ensure that as facilitators of research we enable improved outcomes in research that benefits Indigenous communities.

References

Australian Institute of Aboriginal and Torres Strait Islander Studies (2012). *Guidelines for ethical research in Australian Indigenous studies.* AIATSIS: Canberra.

Australian Linguistic Association (1984). Linguistic rights of Aboriginal and Islander communities. In *The Australian Linguistic Society Newsletter 84(4)*, October 1984.

Byrne, D. R. & Nugent, M. (2004). *Mapping attachment: A spatial approach to Aboriginal post-contact heritage.* Hurstville, NSW: NSW Department of Environment and Conservation.

Cowlishaw, G. (2013). *Australian Aboriginal studies: The anthropologists' accounts.* Canberra: AIATSIS.

Driese, T. & Mazurski, E. (2018). *Weaving knowledges.* Sydney: NSW Department of Aboriginal Affairs.

Federation of Aboriginal and Torres Strait Islander Languages (2004). *FATSIL guide to community protocols for Indigenous language projects.* Sydney: FATSIL.

Hart, V. G. & Whatman, S. L. (1998). Decolonising the concept of knowledge. In *HERDSA: Annual International Conference, July 1998,* 7–10 July 1998, Auckland, New Zealand.

Kar, K. & Chambers, R. (2008). *Handbook on community-led total sanitation.* Brighton: Institute of Development Studies, University of Sussex and Plan UK.

McMahon, S. & McKnight, A. (2020). It's right, wrong, easy and difficult: Learning how to be thoughtful and inclusive of community in research. This volume.

Mooney, J., Riley, L. & Howard-Wagner, D. (2017). *Indigenous online cultural teaching and sharing: Kinship project.* University of Sydney.

Moore, T., Pybus, C., Rolls, M. & Moltow, D. (2017). *Australian Indigenous studies: Research and practice.* Bern: Peter Lang, AG International Academic Publishers.

National Health & Medical Research Council (2003). *Values and ethics: Guidelines for ethical conduct in Aboriginal and Torres Strait Islander health research.* Canberra: Commonwealth of Australia.

National Health & Medical Research Council (2018). Ethical conduct in research with Aboriginal and Torres Strait Islander peoples and communities: Guidelines for researchers and stakeholders. Commonwealth of Australia: Canberra.

National Library of Australia (n.d) *Secret instructions given to Cook.* https://bit.ly/3bnqVlo and https://www.nla.gov.au/content/secret.

NSW Board of Studies (2008). *Working with Aboriginal communities.* Sydney: NSW Board of Studies.

Office of Indigenous Strategy (n.d.) *Aboriginal cultural protocols.* Sydney: Macquarie University.

Popay, J., Escorel, S., Hernandez, M., Johnston, H., Mathieson, J. & Rispel, L. (2008). *Understanding and tackling social exclusion.* World Health Organisation. http://bit.ly/3sZr0S9.

Pascoe, B. (2018). *Dark emu.* Broome: Magabala Books.

Rigney, L-R. (2003). *Indigenous Australian views on knowledge production and Indigenist research.* Canberra: ANU. https://bit.ly/30sLh6d.

Riley-Mundine, L. (2007). Untapping resources for Indigenous students. In Knipe, S. (Ed.) (2007). *Middle years schooling.* Frenchs Forest, NSW: Pearson Education Australia.

Sampson, D., Katrak, M., Rawsthorne, M. & Howard, A. (2020). Way more than a town hall meeting: Connecting with what people care about in community-led disaster planning. This volume.

Sarra, C. (2012). *Good morning Mr Sarra.* St Lucia: University of Queensland Press.

Smith, V. (2010). *Intimate strangers: Friendship, exchange and Pacific encounters.* Cambridge: Cambridge University Press.

Sommerville, M. (2013). Singing the coast: Writing place and identity in Australia. In Johnson, T. & Larsen, S. C. (Eds.). *A deeper sense of place: Stories and journeys of Indigenous–academic collaboration.* Corvallis: Oregon State University Press.

Webster, E., Hill, Y., Hall, A. & See, C. (2020). The Killer Boomerang and other lessons learnt on the journey to undertaking community-led research. This volume.

Welsh, J. & Burgess, C. (2020). Trepidation, trust, and time: Working with Aboriginal communities. This volume.

World Health Organization (2019). *The social determinants of health: Social exclusion.* https://bit.ly/3sZr0S9.

2

Way more than a town hall meeting: connecting with what people care about in community-led disaster planning

Dara Sampson, Meaghan Katrak, Margot Rawsthorne and Amanda Howard

Community-Led Research (CLR) requires processes that support community participation, community prioritising, community decision-making and community action. This chapter sets out to explore the *how* of CLR, or more correctly one key element of the *how*. The particular context for this exploration is community-led disaster resilience building in three communities in New South Wales. The challenging interface in this work between the command-and-control structures of emergency management agencies and more informal community-led processes demonstrates very clearly *how* community-led processes might be supported and hindered.

In particular, we are interested here in how place and space enable or constrain participation, prioritising, decision-making and action in CLR. Key to this interest is an awareness of the importance of disaster preparedness, not only in terms of reducing the impact of the disaster but also in terms of perceived community self-efficacy. We draw on our collective experiences of engaging collaboratively with communities to

D. Sampson, M. Katrak, M. Rawsthorne & A. Howard (2021). Way more than a town hall meeting: Connecting with what people care about in community-led disaster planning. Community-Led Research through an Aboriginal lens. In V. Rawlings, J. Flexner & L. Riley (Eds.), *Community-Led Research: Walking new pathways together*. Sydney: Sydney University Press.

build knowledge for social change, something done through research but also sometimes through community development projects. It is our experience that many of the principles and practices of community development add value to CLR and vice versa. These two fields of practice have the common difficulty of defining 'community', being comfortable with messiness, and requiring long time frames and uncertainty in terms of 'outcomes'. Clarity about values, purpose and processes is foundational for both CLR and community development. What makes this work so challenging but also exciting is how values, purpose and processes are constantly interacting, requiring refining and renegotiating.

Disaster planning cycles of preparedness, response and recovery impact on whole communities, as well as having uneven impacts on particular groups and localities. Recent changes in government-led disaster planning in Australia support a shift from reliance on emergency management agencies as leaders and drivers to one of *shared responsibility* where communities are encouraged to become more self-reliant, working as partners with emergency services (Handmer & McLennan, 2014). Navigating the practicalities of this shift alongside community-led disaster planning reveals the ways in which changing relationships of power and participation between community members and agencies can be more effectively encouraged. This shift also mirrors some of the changes required for research and researchers interested in transitioning from experts to supporters in order to engage with CLR.

It is our experience that often research power relationships are an impediment to building trust and the co-production of new knowledge. Like Pigza (2016), we see community-based research as 'human work that requires time, transparency, authenticity, trust, accountability, and clear communication' (Pigza, 2016, p. 96). Research questions emerge from dialogue and listening, rather than being imposed from outside the community. Community members involved in any research need to have their agency recognised and be able to shape any decisions which are made. Making sure there is a diversity of voices and participation in any research is critical. An ethical responsibility in CLR is that the research itself builds capacity and contributes to the community.

Knowledge building has traditionally sat within university walls. This creates an academic form of knowledge which may not be informed by community practice. A common understanding of universities sees them as 'repositories of sacred knowledge', 'transmitters' of knowledge and 'devoted to discovery' (Moxley, 2003, p. 104). The culture of academia is often elitist, embedding 'expertise' within institutions of higher education (Pigza, 2016). This impacts not only on how individual academics undertake their research but also how the broader community views knowledge building (Powell, 2014). For many, particularly those with fewer resources and opportunities, this can result in an affirmation of academia's claim of ownership of knowledge building. Community-based research is a marked departure from university-initiated research endeavours. For example, the University of Sydney's Strategic Vision included 'a mission to pursue the discovery and dissemination of new knowledge and understanding, attuned to the aspirations of society' (2016, p. 19). This conceptualisation of knowledge building is university-centric, failing to acknowledge or capitalise on the co-production of knowledge. The university hopes to achieve this through investing in research strengths, attracting the best students and, somewhat as an aside, 'expand and develop new partnerships, both locally and globally, that enable our research to make a difference' (University of Sydney, 2016, p. 19). As has been argued previously, this sense in which working beyond the university is not central to knowledge building is not unique to the University of Sydney but common across the academic sector (Carman, 2013; Moxley, 2004; Robinson, 2014).

Growing alternative research approaches which intentionally shift knowledge building, ownership and action is slow, iterative and non-linear. Recalibrating the relationship between communities and traditional knowledge holders such as universities requires patience and goodwill on all sides. The adoption of a community-based research framework (Caine & Mill, 2016; Frankel Merenstein, 2015) to build knowledge *with* residents and others evolves over time. It is supported practically by a range of participatory research methodologies including action research. Like other participatory forms of research (see Stoecker, 2003 for example), community-based research seeks to 'develop practical knowledge that is relevant to the community' (Caine & Mill, 2016, p. 19). Our research activities are grounded in the 'day-to-day experiences of residents and engaged with issues of personal, communal and structural power' (Caine & Mill, 2016, p. 14). Questions arise from the community and reflect issues of importance to the community (Frankel Merenstien, 2015). Through CLR projects knowledge is built about the impact of social policies and programs within a social justice framework that emphasises resident participation in decision-making, community capacity, social inclusion and collaborative action (Vinson & Rawsthorne, 2013; Gilchrist & Taylor, 2011; Rawsthorne & Howard, 2011).

We see CLR as methodologically agnostic, in that it is not predetermined in outcome or approach but driven more by the context and goals of the people we are working with. In the project discussed here, the scope of the data collected supports 'research rigour through triangulation and extended reflection' (Stake, 2003, p. 150). A key focus of this data collection was to 'seek out emic meanings held by the people within the case' (Stake, 2003, p. 144); that is, to explore how individuals interpreted and made sense of their experiences. This agnostic methodological approach is demanding for us as researchers as we need to be able to be competent and flexible across a range of data collection approaches. A community may wish to unpack existing quantitative data (such as the census) or use narrative story telling or arts-informed methodologies to build knowledge about their community. This is unlike more traditional research design approaches where the researcher's skills set, to some extent, shapes the data collection process (think here how often people describe themselves as a 'qualitative' researcher or 'quantitative' researcher or 'mixed methods' researcher). In this way, community-based research can be daunting for the novice researcher. It can also create the opportunity for collaboration among researchers with different skills or preferences, overcoming the need for any one researcher to be the 'jill of all methods'.

As people involved in the creation of knowledge, academics are often viewed as the 'experts' in research theory and methodologies. CLR, of course, disrupts this understanding, with expertise understood as sitting in different places and in different forms. Accessing this knowledge or expertise though is likely to be affected by both place and space. Plainly, community members will feel more able to contribute their knowledge in particular settings and at particular times. To illustrate this, we will draw on recent experiences in CLR with communities preparing for disaster.

Supporting community-led disaster resilience

Since 2018 we have been working in partnership with government, non-government organisations, philanthropic organisations and three communities in New South Wales building community capacities in disaster planning. Integrated with this was an action research process which ran concurrently with activities in each community. An important starting point was that the three communities expressed interest in the project – participation was not top down or imposed from outside, which is too often the experience of communities. The three communities were in very different contexts: peri-urban (this community was located on the outer edges of a major capital city with both rural and expanding urban development); coastal (this community was suburban with a stable population but located in a large tourist region); and remote locations (the last community was a small rural/remote town). The disaster challenges they face are also diverse, including drought, flood, storm and fire. The community-led disaster planning project aimed to support the communities to identify, trial and evaluate locally driven strategies. A participatory action research design was developed for the project which incorporated six action research cycles. The research design included mapping and documenting, learning from each community, supporting knowledge sharing between communities and providing research support for co-designed local disaster-resilience-building initiatives. The research and research team have been clearly located in the project as a resource and support rather than a leader.

In each of the communities, a similar approach was taken to engage with local people and develop ideas for community-led disaster planning, but we found very early that the impacts and follow-on from this process took very different directions in each community. Although the topic of each conversation was focused on *all hazards* disaster resilience (all natural disasters) and the starting point for this conversation was the same, very localised contexts and priorities quickly became the central drivers of community engagement and leadership. For example, in one community, the growing impact of the drought was infused through every local interaction, while in another, the aftermath of a large and devastating cyclone served to amplify existing tensions and gaps in relationships between formal and informal local networks. In each of these cases, planning and action were driven in very different ways by both the places in which community-led planning was emerging, and the spaces in which community members and agencies were able to interact. Historical relationships and narratives of resilience and community connection were quite different in each community, as were existing connections with local emergency services and local government. These factors coalesced throughout the project around the *places* and *spaces* available for participation and community decision-making.

Both of these concepts were central to the ways in which community participation, community prioritising, community decision-making and community action developed.

Place

Conceptually, 'place' is having its day in the sun! Place-based planning, place-based interventions, place-based policy to name just a few. Our use of 'place' here has some similarities with these examples, but we are also drawing on the sociological understanding of belonging through and in place (Bennett, 2015). In the community development literature, 'places gain meaning through social interactions and are far more than simply geographic locations' (Plunkett et al., 2018, p. 473). Plunkett and colleagues argue that 'a place is created when people assign meaning to previously undistinguished spaces' (2018, p. 473). On a similar line, Bennett argues 'belonging as a way of being-in-the-world is less tangible but *becomes tangible through relationships with place*, things and other people, that create it and result from it' (2015, p. 956, emphasis added). Community life (at the nexus of the social and the physical environment) is given its shape through the 'habitual use of a place by the people who inhabit it' (Bennett, 2015, p. 956).

Place shapes how community members engage with community-led processes, be these development or research oriented. As our title suggests, CLR requires 'way more than a town hall meeting'. In the three communities, we repeatedly noted the impact of place on who was in the room, whose voice was valued and who was absent. The usual places for formal community gatherings – town halls, community centres, etc. – attracted people already networked into these formal places. These 'tried and true' places limited community participation to the 'tried and true' performance. Community members will belong to or be excluded from these places – 'through an attachment to place created over time, intersubjective relationships to others in the place and inalienable relationships to the materiality of the place' (Bennett, 2015, p. 956). For knowledge building, this formality of place created a focus on 'representative samples' and 'surveys'. Such an approach, in our experience, has limited transformational possibilities. Community needs may be documented (often thoroughly) through this process, but reports are then left on shelves to gather dust. In this performance, research is seen as an end in itself – there is little understanding or engagement with research as being a (contested) knowledge claim. The power of 'place' in Community-led processes was evident when conversations were held in informal or unusual places.

The irony of inclusion is that many of our formal processes aimed at inclusion are experienced as very exclusionary. A public meeting in which 'all are welcome' advertised through local media, held at the town hall on a Thursday evening, might on the surface appear inclusive but in fact creates multiple barriers to participation. These formal meetings were dominated by people representing agencies or particular interests. In one community, Aboriginal community members only became involved when conversations shifted away from these formal processes. Meeting in places familiar and safe to the Aboriginal community saw greater participation, transforming the project away from service-system and information-heavy responses. In this community, a number of smaller conversations exploring possibilities and connections between knowledge of Country,[1] community relationships

---

1   Country is an Aboriginal English (as different from Standard Australian English) term that describes land as a living entity, the essence of Aboriginality and includes the people, culture, spirituality, history, environment etc.

and the importance and value of culture in disaster-resilience building led to participation in a broader conversation. Similar listening and connecting conversations were held at the local pub, annual show and local shops before a wider community meeting was experienced as valuable and inclusive. Through informal conversations, innovations and creative collaborations emerged that were unique to the context.

In other communities, local businesses such as cafes and pubs emerged as places in which very constructive community conversations could occur. These are natural bump zones where community members mix across differences that might otherwise divide them. The community places people use in everyday life have been the places where community-led ideas have been incubated into projects and initiatives ready to be shared with the wider community before further refinement and adaption. In all three communities (although in different ways) where community members were able to shift the conversation from a more compartmentalised and service-driven frame – for example, information provision for disaster responses – to one which included all aspects of community life in particular places, community members joined and stayed with the emerging projects.

In the communities, understandings of and relationships to *place* included social, cultural, economic and environmental aspects. Community-led decision-making integrated these aspects throughout deliberations and in action. In one community, it was only after key community members came to understand that the focus of the project was much broader than flooding that other community members came on board, and more inclusive ideas for long-term, and community -wide, resilience-building came together. Often research projects prioritise reducing the scope and focus for manageability. In CLR, one learning from this project is that processes which recognise the intersections of community life rather than compartmentalising these provide a better fit with community experiences and perceptions.

In the particular communities involved in this project, *place* was experienced as *all aspects of where I live and where I belong.* CLR had limited success until community members were able to shape resilience-building projects that reflected this understanding of community life. This took time and also a process of making *space* for genuine community participation, deliberation and decision-making. We now turn to this element of *space* in our exploration of the *how* of CLR. Layered with *place*, the ways in which *spaces* are constructed, opened up and maintained resulted in very different levels of community participation and sustained engagement in the community sites.

The concept of *space*, in a community development context, is both a physical and an abstract one. It is physical in its relationship to *place* – how, if at all, does the physical environment invite or hinder participation? There is an intimate connection between place and space. The concepts of power and place are linked in that the choice of venue, time and the general parameters of a collective gathering inherently privilege some participants over others. This power is the more abstract element of *space*. How space is used, filled (or not) in a physical sense will influence space in a relational sense. As space can be created for participation, it can also be used (often unconsciously) to exclude participation. This understanding of how to use space is a nuanced skill and requires facilitators and researchers to be highly emotionally aware of people, power and social inclusion (and exclusion). It requires knowledge of these dynamics and a skill and preparedness to create space and safety for lesser-heard voices. This seems like a clear and well-known process in community engagement and development; however, we found in this project that knowledge and practice were often more challenging to integrate. Two quotes below illustrate the ways in which community members navigated and made sense of the means by which space could be used to challenge and include:

> I am enjoying seeing that some tenants are very involved in this project and that they're energised by it. That they're having a voice in it which is great and I'd like to see that continue.
>
> [Emergency services] are coming at it from a point of view – look at the plans, everything's fine, it all works, they are saying, 'Yes, it all works'. But you know what, having the residents there to actually say, 'We don't really care if it works'. This is still our concern. I think that was good to have.

In the first quote, the community member notes the value and importance of making space for community members to be involved; and in the second, the importance of advocacy and valuing alternative views is articulated. In both quotes, we see spaces made and utilised actively by community members and these voices are central to CLR.

In the community-led disaster planning research we observed the complexity of valuing contributions from highly engaged and active community members (the people eager to be at the town hall meeting), whilst also endeavouring to hear the quieter (or absent) voices. This was keenly highlighted in one particular community, where initial workshop participants came from a neighbouring and well-connected community. Community members from this community were small in number and initially the louder voices from the neighbouring area focused discussion on their community. *Space* was unintentionally shut down for the small number of local voices in the community. *Space* for community voices were excluded further from the project discussion when the low attendance of these residents was attributed to there being no community in the local area. Central to this closing down of *space* was the community engagement facilitator's understanding of community itself. Low attendance at the workshop or town hall meeting of local people was explained as a community problem rather than a problem for the community engagement process. *Space* for community participation and deliberation was refocused into a neighbouring community with the local community excluded because they did not attend the town hall meeting. This assumption that in order to participate interested communities will attend the *space* which is set up by those outside the community, is one that workers and researchers should be aware of as it imposes a top-down planning process.

Shevellar and Westoby (2018) outline key principles normative to community development relevant to this discussion of *space*. Two of these principles are of direct relevance to this discussion in that they underpin the ideology of Community-Led disaster preparedness and research. First, the concept of social justice 'working towards betterment, emancipation and empowerment, equity, social justice, self-determination and the re-allocation of resources to the greatest social benefit' (Shevellar & Westoby, 2018, p. 5). The second principle of note is valuing local knowledge and resources. How inclusive and exclusive *spaces* were opened up and shut down in this process directly impacted the way these principles could be enacted. *Spaces* are a central shaper in terms of who has voice and power. Here, deliberation *space* is cordoned off for those who follow the processes set up and run by those outside the community. Community members who did not follow expectations (to attend the meeting) were unintentionally made invisible. They did not attend so they did not exist.

Later in the project, re-engagement with the focus community using the strategies described above – cafe meetings, spending time at the local farmers' market, connecting with community members in everyday life – resulted in a very different group of people meeting together at the local pub to explore and develop ideas that were priorities for them. This group comprised only residents of the community. When the discussion re-centred around that community, local people joined the planning process. In part this can also be attributed to the framing of the issue, namely the scope and magnitude of disasters and their impact on people. How questions are asked is vitally important.

The concept of the 'wicked problem' (Bishop & Dzidic, 2014) (describing complex problems, seemingly intractable and unresolvable) bears consideration in this project because 'both the problems and solutions are confounding, with outcomes often ambiguous' (Shevellar & Westoby, 2018 p. 4). One of the tensions created throughout this project was the 'push/pull' between exploration of the issues and a propensity to try to 'solve' the community needs. Again, when this is done by outside workers not part of a community, ownership and self-determination are placed at risk. Space for community connection, deliberation and decision-making are constrained.

From the perspective of community members, *space* for community deliberation, exploration of issues and ideas and decision-making was further shut down when discussions were funding-led. In one community, time and space was made for community members to talk, connect and slowly develop ideas and initiatives which they could start with already existing resources. Only after this, they began to explore project expansion and the possibility of funding. In the community described above, community-led planning workshops led with the promise of funding and this both skewed and constrained spaces for considered discussion and resulted in a longer process of community engagement.

As part of some snapshot data collection in the project, the research team conducted phone interviews with a sample of participants from this particular community who had been invited to be involved in the community-led disaster planning project.

Through the course of these interviews, it became apparent community members and organisation staff held differing motivations for being involved in the project, which also bore a relationship to their ongoing involvement. For those who attended the initial workshop in the coastal community, including representatives from the neighbouring community, the promise of funding was seen as a major motivator. In addition, it became clear at meetings that different members of the community held differing views as to the most effective use of any funds. This created a competitive rather than a deliberative dynamic in meetings, which constrained space for a slower and more inclusive conversation. People came to the workshop with a ready-made project and in order to seek funds. Local community members were, as a result, crowded out by established groups and organisations outside the community. What is of interest in facilitating community-led projects is the tendency for funds to take over the conversation and to be seen as the panacea for all ills. The unintended consequence of this is disempowerment for participants, as the focus shifts from community strengths and ideas to external solutions, pre-designed projects and organisationally oriented goals.

This dovetailed into clarity of purpose for the project. In particular, there was confusion as to the role of the project staff and that of the research team (and action research). This is worthy of consideration for future projects undertaken with this approach as the 'faces' (for community members) largely became merged and the people remembered were the most recent people to have been present. Purpose was also enmeshed in the discussion above about the goals of the project.

A final learning from the research about the importance of space relates to diversity and participation. Those who attended the first workshop (the town hall meeting) from the community felt disenfranchised and that their goals had not been met. A community-led planning process here might take time to engage with a broader group in the community and support the small group who attended to collaborate in this process. The workshop or town hall meeting process both heightened the *space* for this group to be the sole community representatives but simultaneously shut down *spaces* for their voice to be effectively heard and for this group to work on a broader engagement plan. Their voice was marginalised unintentionally because they were seen as both not representative of the whole community (due to small numbers) and as a symbol that the community did not exist in this particular place. Only later in the project was the *space* for a more inclusive conversation with this group and other local community members opened up.

For others who had either chosen not to be involved in the project or who had withdrawn after the first meeting there was a sense of not having had a voice. It is an issue worthy of reflection in relation to how the creation of space and the use of place might have influenced this belief and how space and place could be used differently in future.

The ways in which the contours of *space* in this particular community changed the dynamics of community participation and opportunities for community members to work together on local initiatives were significant.

Observation of the use of both *place* and *space* in this project has provided us with an opportunity to reflect on the values which underpin community-led work and research. The term itself (community) holds different meanings for different people. It is not always clear if community is an inherent concept or something we create, and whether it is prescribed by ourselves or with others (Meade, Shaw & Banks, 2016). Politically, 'community' contains notions of democracy, reciprocity and self-determination but it can also enhance (or create) difference and exclusion (Bauman, 2001). Inherent in the concept of community-led work is a conscious deconstruction of traditional paradigms of working with people that can both assume and reinforce or create traditional power paradigms. Traditional models of community development and research have assumed knowledge is held with the 'expert' (be it the worker or the researcher). Inverting this assumption and working from an egalitarian premise provides rich experiences but brings its own ethical challenges.

One of these ethical challenges arose in the conduct of this project and it relates to the underpinning (and differing) value sets of the key stakeholders. Looking around the town hall at community meetings, it became clear the issues mentioned of *space* and *place* arose from different expectations and values.

Emergency services have long held the mantle of responsibility and authority in the disaster *space*. With responsibility and authority comes power, whether this is a known power or (even) a wanted power. Changing the relationships between emergency services and communities is a slow and uneven process. Like researchers, emergency services are caught between the imperative to take charge, the expectations of communities that they will, and the understanding that this position is unsustainable and disempowering for communities. Interestingly, in the communities where clear boundaries and parameters for negotiation between community members and agencies have been established early, opportunities have been created for emergency services to adopt a supportive rather than leading role. This shows promise as a practice for realigning relationships of power and expertise and establishing sustainable community-led planning. The two quotes below provide some examples of this thinking and the ways in which goodwill was enacted to build collaboration:

> Look, I think it was definitely a good way to have the committee structured. I've been involved in a couple of other ones with a similar focus but without that sort of broad scope of residents, local community groups being involved, and I definitely saw the benefit of that. Taking that whole community approach has got to be the way forward and I think that is probably the biggest thing that I've taken from it and look, if we could do that every time that we have to get out there and do something in the public and have communities involved and getting them to take the lead and taking some responsibility for it, great.

> Anything to do with fostering sort of disaster preparedness in the community has got to be community-led and it's got to be done in collaboration. It can't just be us going in saying, 'Here's what you need to do.' We need to do it in collaboration.

In this project, key learning about CLR, in a similar way, has highlighted the importance of researchers supporting rather than leading community knowledge building. We have seen most success where communities have sought their own *space* in this first instance, to think, listen, plan and design. This *space* has not been free of tension, but deliberations, negotiations and consensus building have been more successful when community members have been able to open up and maintain that *space*, inviting agencies and researchers in when needed as supporters and collaborators. *Place* is defined by community members and *space* is created to talk through and act on all aspects of community life, of which resilience-building for disasters is just one element.

References

Bauman, Z. (2001). *Community: Seeking safety in an insecure world.* Cambridge: Polity Press.

Bennett, J. (2015). 'Snowed in!': Offbeat rhythms and belonging as everyday practice. *Sociology, 49*(5), pp. 955–969.

Bishop, B. J. & Dzidic, P. L. (2014). Dealing with wicked problems: Conducting a causal layered analysis of complex social psychological issues. *American Journal of Community Psychology, 53*, pp. 13–24.

Caine, V. & Mill, J. (2016). *Essentials of community-based research.* Oxon: Routledge.

Carman, M. (2013). Research impact: The gap between commitment and implementation systems in national and institutional policy in Australia. *The Australasian Journal of University-Community Engagement, 8(2)*, pp. 1–14.

Frankel Merenstien, B. (2015). Community-based research methods: Putting ideas into action. *Journal of Applied Society Science, 9(2)*, pp. 125–138.

Handmer, J. & McLennan, B. (2014). *Sharing responsibility in Australian disaster management: Final report.* Melbourne: Bushfire Co-operative Research Centre, RMIT University.

Howard, A. & Rawsthorne, M. (2019) *Everyday community practice: Principles and practice.* Crows Nest, NSW: Allen & Unwin.

Meade, R., Shaw, M. & Banks, S. (2016). Politics, power and community development: An introductory essay. In R. Meade, M. Shaw & S. Banks (Eds.), *Politics, power and community development*, pp. 1–27. Bristol: Policy Press Scholarship.

Moxley, D. (2003). Books in higher education and their implications for community practice. *Journal of Community Practice, 11*(3), pp. 103–111.

Moxley, D. (2004). Engaged research in higher education and civic responsibility reconsidered. *Journal of Community Practice, 12*(3–4), pp. 235–242.

Pigza, J. (2016). The POWER model: Five core elements for teaching community-based research. In M. Beckman & J. Long (Eds.), *Community-based research: Teaching for community impact*, pp. 93–107. Sterling, VA: Stylus Publishing.

Plunkett, D., Phillips, R. & Ucar Kocaoglu, B. (2018). Place attachment and community development. *Journal of Community Practice, 26*(4), pp. 471–482, DOI: 10.1080/10705422.2018.1521352.

Powell, K. (2014). In the shadow of the ivory tower: An ethnographic study of neighbourhood relations. *Qualitative Social Work, 13*(1), pp. 108–126.

Rawsthorne, M. & Howard, A. (2011). *Working with communities: Critical perspectives*. Champaign, Ill.: Common Ground Publishing.

Robinson, P. (2014). Identifying best practice in university community engagement. Unpublished. Sydney: Glebe Community Development Project.

Shevellar, L. & Westoby, P. (2018). Wicked problems and community development. In L. Shevellar & P. Westoby (Eds.), *The Routledge handbook of community development research*, pp. 1–17. London: Taylor & Francis.

Stake, R. (2003). Case studies. In Denzin, N. K & Lincoln, Y. (Eds.), *Strategies for qualitative enquiry*, pp. 134–164. Thousand Oaks, CA: Sage Publications.

Stoecker, R. (2003). *Liberating service learning and the rest of higher education civic engagement*. Philadelphia: Temple University Press.

University of Sydney (2016). If you change nothing, nothing will change. *Strategic Plan 2016–2020*. Sydney: University of Sydney. https://bit.ly/3v6NRNI.

Vinson, T. & Rawsthorne, M. (2013). *Lifting our gaze: The community appraisal and strengthening framework*. Champaign, Ill.: Common Ground Publishing.

3

It's right, wrong, easy and difficult: learning how to be thoughtful and inclusive of community in research

Samantha McMahon and Anthony McKnight

This chapter reflects on our lived experiences of data analysis and writing processes for producing one particular journal article titled 'No shame at AIME' (McKnight et al., 2019). AIME is the Australian Indigenous Mentoring Experience; it is a not-for-profit, educational mentoring program that 'builds mentoring bridges between universities and schools' (aimementoring.com, 2019) for educationally disadvantaged young people. Within the lens of Community-Led Research (CLR), we rethink the role of community in the process we used in preparing the 'No shame at AIME' research article; we tease out who was leading whom throughout the research process and how undertaking this work in a university context affected the process and outcomes.

This is a philosophical paper, which draws on McKnight's (2017) work on tripartation. Tripartation helped us to place Country in relationship with our experiences of CLR. The way this helped us was to utilise and connect to trees. In this way we do not just use the trees as a metaphor but as a way to explore and explain our learning from Country. Tripartation is finding spiritual connections to concepts,

S. McMahon & A. McKnight (2021). It's right, wrong, easy and difficult: Learning how to be thoughtful and inclusive of community in research. In V. Rawlings, J. Flexner & L. Riley (Eds.), *Community-Led Research: Walking new pathways together*. Sydney: Sydney University Press.

things or situations that are often viewed as separate or distinctive and different from each other, which is represented by the tilde (~) and replaces the more common use of the forward slash (/). For example, the tree/human binary is where we are seen as being separate; however, trees~humans both hold water in our bodies, we both need oxygen and carbon dioxide, plus we live in family groups and community. We use the tilde quite deliberately in this article to philosophise the connections in a variety of concepts and issues under discussion.

This chapter is organised in two broad moves. First, we paint a landscape of trees and describe their relationships with each other as nature, then we articulate how the academy (manifested as academics, universities and commercial publishing houses) serve as arborists to reshape what the tree and its community should be like.

Trees live in communities

> Trees live in tribes, just like people. (Harrison & McConchie, 2009, p. 139)

Human beings live in communities and so do trees. Both authors of this chapter recognise the communities that they belong to that have informed their experiences of working on the 'No shame at AIME' paper. The communities we are connected to are multiple. Each of these communities share similarities, differences and overlaps. We exist at the intersections of many communities. To support our thinking around community, McHugh, Coppola, Holt and Anderson's (2015) research on examining the meaning of community from urban Aboriginal youth identified community as:

> belonging, supportive interactions, family and friends, sport, and where you live and come from ... Participants acknowledged that they are part of various communities (e.g. First Nation community, school community) and, therefore, this notion of multiple communities is a common thread that spans all themes. (p. 79)

Although this particular study relates to young people's experience of community through sport, this concept of community very closely aligns with our own understandings and approaches to CLR. However, our working understandings of community extend from this to acknowledge Country as key to our communities.

In our 'No shame at AIME' paper we used Rose's (1996) description of the term Country, which describes Country as:

> multi-dimensional – it consists of people, animals, plants, Dreamings, underground, earth, soils, minerals, surface water, and air. There is sea country and land country; in some areas people talk about sky country. Country has origins and a future; it exists both in and through time … (p. 8).

From one author's (McKnight's) relationship with Uncle Max Harrison (Yuin Elder), we have in our research always included the communities that make up Country (trees, animals and so on) into our thinking on community. Thereby, we share belonging to numerous communities on the South Coast of New South Wales; for example, the community of insects, mammals, birds and trees and the communities such as Nowra, Wollongong and the university. However, our relationships with other communities are different – for example, the Aboriginal author's connection to the Aboriginal community. Anthony McKnight is an Awabakal, Gumaroi and Yuin man, and also has British heritage from his father's family. Anthony is a father, husband, uncle, son, grandson, brother, cousin, nephew, friend and cultural man. Samantha's family heritage is from Ireland, Scotland and Wales. Samantha and Anthony both teach in preservice teacher education and collaborate to contribute to decolonising the educational research space.

Both have written together before and work from their own knowledge systems to challenge each other's thinking on an issue of educational in~equality. The entity that connects us both and the other authors of the 'No shame' paper is Yuin Country,[1] which provides us with everything we need to live. We are human beings that are part of

---

1   Yuin Country 'extends from the Snowy River in the South to the escarpment of Wollongong, our northern boundary, and then out to the Southern

a broader community, which is Country. We recognise Yuin Country and Yuin Country's contribution to the 'No shame' paper; moreover, its ongoing contribution through trees that help us reflect and think here. The team responsible for the 'No shame' paper are thinkers, who, ironically, are not also co-authoring this chapter: Valerie Harwood, Jake Trindorfer, Amy Priestly and Uncle Max Dulamumun Harrison. We say this not to be glib but to position ourselves as recounting our experiences, not those of all in our writing community. In this sense, what we write here is in no way generalisable to the experiences of others involved. This chapter specifically reflects on our journey (McKnight and McMahon).

The other way we can view this research conundrum is that it is very simple. Not simple as in artless or easy but simple in that the issues can be identified, discussed and resolved if each interconnecting issue is unpacked as it arises: time is required to do this respectfully. The issue may take time to arise, as may the resolution, which might have to take numerous forms, as the heart of the matter is the matter of concern: the heart. When a heart is involved, patience is required and the heart here is Country. In this sense our focus is on Aboriginal students who are Country. 'I am placed, therefore I am' (Mary Graham cited in Rose 2004, p. 189). Therefore, our research paper 'No shame' had to be placed with Country and the students, and at the same time with a community organisation that we worked with to do the research. As the relationships took time to develop, so did the paper.

Communities of trees: notions of leadership as reciprocity

We are prompted to ask the question of CLR, who's leading whom through data analysis and writing and should it always be a hierarchical and sustained relationship? In a community of trees there is no hierarchy of leadership as each member will have a time to lead, to follow and to be in between both. Older trees will support younger trees in or over time, and vice versa. The hard part is to know when you need

Tablelands. Our Country follows the coast down and into Victoria' (Harrison & McConchie, 2009, p. 15).

to take a leadership role, when to follow and when to be in between. By in between, we mean you take your role in the process that is required for it to function as a community of researchers connected to Country. Therefore, learning how to be reciprocal in this dynamic is an essential element that unfolds in its own way, which can also be hard and/or easy. In either way, how the process unfolds can be right or wrong, with this all depending upon the relationships to communicate if it is too hard or easy for the team.

The central idea of this chapter rests on troubling the Western idea of what 'leadership' is as it appears in scholarship from the United Kingdom, Canada, America, Australia and New Zealand. To us, community leadership is not simply inverting a hierarchical relationship between the researcher and the researched. This is not to say that we think Western theorisation of leadership rests entirely in ideas of hero-leaders, individual leaders and personal leadership qualities. We are aware that in the 21st-century ideas of leadership as distributed and/or shared have come to proliferate (e.g. Bush, 2013; Lumby, 2013; Youngs, 2017). Distributed leadership was introduced by Spillane and colleagues in 2004:

> Leadership practice [is] constituted in the interaction among these [leaders and followers]. There was also a reciprocal relationship between the practice of these leaders. Each required input from the others to facilitate the activity. In such *reciprocal interdependencies*, individuals play off one another, with the practice of person A enabling the practice of person B, and vice versa. Hence, what A does can only be fully understood by taking into account what B does and vice versa. Such collective leading depends on multiple leaders working together, each bringing somewhat different resources, skills and knowledge to bear. (Spillane, Halverson & Diamond, 2004, p. 18, original emphasis)

However, over time this approach has been critiqued (e.g. Lumby, 2013) and taken in different directions. We recognise touching points between our experiences of CLR and Spillane and colleagues' notion of reciprocal interdependencies between leaders and leaders working together in complementary ways. However, this is not completely transferable in its entirety to our CLR practice. We prefer to use Grice's (2019) deployment of Stephen Kemmis and colleagues' work to produce a more nuanced (and we think appropriate) interpretation and move away from owners of 'leadership' to co-constructed 'leading':

> Leading can differently be defined as practice ... This definition is critical, because leading takes the emphasis away from titled people and instead studies the practices that occur in the intersubjective spaces between people from their 'sayings, doings and relatings'. (Grice, 2019, p. 58)

In our thinking and writing on Yuin Country, in Australia, in writing the 'No shame' paper, we consciously worked to avoid responsibilising and owning 'leaders' and 'leadership'. What we did, we believe, is more in line with Grice's (2019) argument of focusing on the action of co-creating 'leading'. Whilst this description of leading is close to our practice of CLR, we don't adopt any one notion of leadership from Western scholarship as complete because none that we found significantly drew on Indigenous ways of knowing, being and doing leadership~following. Moreover, whilst distributed and shared leadership literature pays special attention to context, Country is more than context and doesn't 'fit' such theorisations – we need a different way to explain our experiences of CLR. We needed a way to show what it means to follow Country's leadership in the research process; in this way, 'following' can also be understood as leading and sustaining a legacy role of taking care, for example, of trees.

Reflecting on our experiences, we identify that like an ecology and community of trees, leadership was fluid and involved oscillating between taking leadership and following responsibilities. We had to ask ourselves the question, which can often be hard, 'Is it my turn to step up or to stay put and listen?' This question focused the gaze at self, recognising capacities from moment to moment to learn and to contribute based on skills and positionality and a shared value of reciprocity.

The term reciprocation (see also chapters by Riley & Webster et al., this volume) was imperative in our partnerships between the Aboriginal organisation that led the research at various stages to find points of connection from AIME's protocols, our institutions and Country. Reciprocation is not just towards humans; it is with all the communities that make up Country. As Jo-Ann Archibald (1997), a First Nation woman from the Sto:lo First Nation in British Columbia, Canada, explains, reciprocation is 'to be in harmony with oneself, others, members of the animal kingdom and other elements of nature [and] requires that First Nations people respect the gifts of each entity and establish and maintain respectful reciprocal relations with each' (p. 78). This worldview on reciprocation in research processes could cause yet another layer of confusion for non-Indigenous researchers engaging in CLR. Therefore, as Gray and Oprescu (2016) argue from an Indigenous health research position, 'It is important that non-Indigenous researchers become more aware of culturally safe ways in which to undertake Indigenous research and ensure that the research undertaken is appropriate, ethical and useful for participants' (p. 464). When Indigenous peoples are connected to Country (the overall entity that births the gifting entities), being reciprocal and ethical in research from an Indigenous holistic manner, it is not only appropriate but essential to keep the relationships safe between all of the givers of gifts. This journey of working towards a respectful reciprocal research relationship and partnership that is safe with an Aboriginal organisation is often seen as a very complex issue. This research dynamic within the Western knowledge system could well be argued as complex with the competing nature and historical context of colonial practice, knowledge, processes and structural frameworks. To keep something safe a person with a good heart is required – a heart that takes care of Country – and a memory that can go back before the Industrial Revolution.

Processes of sharing leadership and reciprocity don't function purely on an intellectual level; we are not advocating here simply for a to-do list split equitably according to 'research' and 'community' expertise. Genuine sharing and reciprocity of research leadership between research team members requires heart – an emotional investment in the purpose and value of the research undertaking and of each other. The heart has, and is, a memory (personal communication with Uncle Max Harrison, 2016). When this association between the heart and mind is understood from an Aboriginal way of knowing, the effects of colonisation and colonising and hierarchical research practices can function to obscure cultural understandings of reciprocal leadership, being and doing – as in the trees. If a Western knowledge system removes heart via insistence on traditional hierarchical research relationships (community – or researcher-led or otherwise), for Aboriginal people involved in the research it could have the effect of burying a heart and a memory. And this burying of heart and memory would restrict genuine responsibilities and capacities to take turns leading the research process. Ireland (2009) presents a First Nation Canadian worldview on the importance of heart to people's learning spirit, as the heart is connected to the mind and body and is then a constant guide for a person in becoming who they are meant to be.

Any research relationship with heart includes a range of emotions and actions and can be understood by the term love. Love, according to Uncle Max Harrison, is 'lots of varying emotions' (personal communication, 2014). Doing the research, writing and review experience for the 'No shame' paper, we went through lots of varying emotions, in the same way that many academics do in their work, whether or not they believe they are doing community-led~reciprocal research. In the 'No shame' paper, our shared 'heart' was the protection of Aboriginal students in schools and cultural understandings of shame (baambi and baambi-mumm).[2] By this we mean that our heart guided authorship to share knowledge that could assist schools and teachers to actively work to make schools less shameful and more inclusive places for Aboriginal students. This heart also included an explicit effort to 'unbury' and 'unobscure' cultural understandings and memories of shame in colonial schooling contexts and academia.

Members of the authoring team brought their own knowledge, heart and memory. In addition to shared heart for the paper, we brought unique hearts that needed to take turns in contributing to the paper's development. This turn-taking, we suggest, is another example of research leadership as reciprocation. Reciprocation is all to do with

---

2   With permission from Uncle Max, the first word for shame in lore is baambi (strength in holding lore), while the second word (everyday use) is baambi-mumm (scared, frightened). A fuller explanation is within McKnight et al. (2019).

the relationship that exists with all of the participants that are in our story – humans, trees and other entities from Country that hold knowledge. This relationship is complex because it does not want to be looked at in the easy, hard, right, wrong manner. The simplicity from an Aboriginal position is the relationship and identifying something that brings every living thing together: Country. Which leads us to a question: what are the core issues from Country that help the complex issues to become not only simple but an achievable pathway for each issue in the relationship to be healed? For us that is time, respect and trees, especially the heart of a tree: it takes time for a tree to grow and the respect we give that tree for it to grow. Kids took up 'No shame at AIME' often in interviews. They took a leadership role to initiate this.

What is the role of an arborist? The university, academic freedom and economic rationalism shaping the community of trees

What we found was our enactment of CLR was not a model of community-always-leading-the-process, as the CLR title might otherwise suggest. Nor was it simply a matter of leadership being distributed; there was no central leader 'allowing' others to do leading roles (Lumby, 2013). The notion of community always leading was constrained via processes of co-creating leading with many leaders; leading and following positions were always and ever in respectful movement and flux throughout the process. To illustrate this, we recount in this short list below how leadership 'moved' from tree to tree:

1. AIME led the research by commissioning the independent evaluation and articulating what they wanted to know from that evaluation.
2. Funding bodies led (Australian Department of Education and Training), building parameters around project costs, spending, personnel and key performance indicators.
3. Researchers led consultations with AIME to support research design, instrument development, and ethics application phases of the project that would 'fit in' and not interrupt normal program delivery.

4. AIME and researchers worked co-operatively to organise and undertake fieldwork, respectively.

5. AIME students (mentees) led discussions of 'No shame at AIME'. There were no questions about 'No shame at AIME' in the interview schedules, but students kept initiating conversations about this during semi-structured interviews.

6. Researchers led organisation of data analysis with AIME staff (two Indigenous and one non-Indigenous) and Indigenous education scholar and local Lawman (McKnight).

7. University financial services led rigorous objections to researchers spending money on accommodation and food for a four-day data analysis retreat. Conventional qualitative data analysis only costs academics' time (or the money spent paying research assistants to manage datasets and run analyses).

8. Researchers led appeals to finance to make a sound case for a need to spend project money on a data analysis retreat that would bring researchers, AIME and community into conversation to develop shared and culturally appropriate interpretations of the 'No shame at AIME' data, which had thus far only been collected and thought through by non-Indigenous researchers.

9. University financial services led the approval process that made spending money for the retreat possible.

10. Country (and AIME staff) led data analysis; this process was facilitated by McKnight. This analysis process focused on developing shared and culturally informed understandings of (i) existing literature about shame in Aboriginal cultures and in Australian educational contexts and (ii) data collected during six months of national fieldwork regarding 'No shame at AIME' (for example, student interviews and researchers' classroom observation notes).

11. Leadership oscillated between (i) researchers (McKnight, Country, McMahon, Harwood) preparing text and (ii) AIME authors (Priestly and Trindorfer) leading feedback on revisions, prompting further revisions, and authorising subsequent and final revisions.

12. Researchers led submission to journals.

13. Journal editorial boards and reviewers led article revision processes in terms of previous editions of the journal, setting patterns of

preferred ways of constructing journal article texts and providing feedback about the work needed to shift and change in order to appeal to their readership.

14. Country and researchers (McKnight et al.) led rewriting the article in response to reviews.

15. Uncle Max Dulamunmun Harrison led the clarification around knowledge contested by the reviewer that there is no Aboriginal word for shame.

16. *Australian Journal of Indigenous Education* led publication of the article via their journal scope and sequence, the expertise of their reviewing panel and their publication proficiency.

17. Academics continue to lead through citations of the published work.

To have community 'lead' each move in the above list of research processes would be neither desirable nor ethical. If we consider non-community people in the research process as arborists that constrain~enable the larger community-led project (the community of trees) we can come to see non-community elements of CLR as necessary-destructive.

> Trees live in tribes just like people. When a tree is born and then it is moved to another area, for whatever reason, that's like taking a person out of their country and putting them in a different country. They are like refugees. (Harrison & McConchie, 2009, p. 139)

Human beings live in communities and so do trees. Therefore, when trees have been moved and then groomed by humans (arborists) you are damaging responsibility and independent behaviour that is respectful to maintain a community. The human needs are put above another community member, the tree, which affects/has effects on the human community. The trick for researchers involved in community-led projects is to discern when 'stepping up' into leadership positions is more a help than a hindrance and in ways that do not remove or relocate the trees.

Arguably, *researchers should lead* when their expertise will save community time, effort and frustration (for example, ethics applications, funding reports, submitting journal articles, arguing with finance departments). Likewise, to have researchers lead uniformly throughout this process would have been unethical and disrespectful of the community's voices, needs and wants.

One way of understanding the necessity of these tensions involved in community leading and not leading research is to think using the story~theory of tripartation. Tripartation includes the spiritual dynamic so we can engage in knowing on a mind, body and spiritual level that is in oneness. Tripartation for McKnight is the spiritual umbilical cord that can connect binaries/dualities, instead of the Western binary that tends to separate (McKnight, 2015). Importantly, time is required to know, be and do this within research on the physical, mental and spiritual realms, which are not meant to be separated. Therefore, it is necessary to be aware of contradictions and utilise them to assist in the reduction in doing and being in research in a way that is respectful to both knowledge systems. Tripartation enabled our understanding of CLR as a number of contradictions (in terms of partioscillating and reciprocal leadership between many parties), and utilising a two-knowledge approach. It provided space in our thinking to identify, explain what we could, and to be aware that we struggled and missed some elements amongst the difficulties and benefits of researching in two knowledge systems.

The process of using tripartation as a way of 'doing' CLR requires patience to allow time for spirit to come through. Patience can contribute to reducing the immediacy effect of Western knowledge, which can restrict Aboriginal knowledge approaches that are full of silence to see Country talk without voice (Harrison & McConchie, 2009; McKnight, 2015). This includes the community having time to deliberate as a community of knowledge holders. This did and can include non-Aboriginal people if they are allowed to have the time to do the learning within the research context. The importance of time is a constant theme throughout this edited volume. Using the above list of times and spaces where different people led the 'Community-Led' Research and to show how this turn-taking enabled-restrained, and made easy and difficult, we offer now an elaboration of one item on the list – point 15.

For example (at point 15 in the list above), regarding conversations with community members, we can talk specifically about one conversation led by Uncle Max when responding to a reviewer's assertion that there was no Aboriginal word for shame. Using tripartation, we can see these things in relationship as at once constraining~enabling. When reviewers led with negative and what seemed unhelpful assertions that there was no Aboriginal word for shame, this both constrained the progress of the article to publication but also enabled us to ask better questions in our conversations with Uncle Max and to seek old answers. Likewise, our conversation with Uncle Max enabled new learning for us, a path forward to publication and ways to recognise constrictions in our own thinking (that is, just because we can't see or don't know something doesn't mean it is not there). This conversation also worked to constrain the power of the reviewer's criticisms levelled at us. In working in this space of constraint-enabling and using tripartation, we avoided making either the reviewer or Uncle Max or ourselves right or wrong. In this moment of CLR it was right~wrong, easy~difficult, enabled~constrained. But this process took time and patience, with an overarching practice of respect for all involved.

To further explain the importance of time (timing), and to show how researchers can be followers, we tell a brief 'back-story' about this conversation with Uncle Max. We had submitted to a journal and received a really negative review. One of the authors (Harwood) had recommended that we delay preparing any response to this until after McKnight had submitted his PhD. In hindsight, this was an important temporal break. When we did sit down to prepare a response, the researchers were not leading but were following the thinking prompts provided by the reviewer: that there was no Aboriginal word for shame. The timing of this conversation with Uncle Max was pivotal. We spoke with him only two days after he got a memory (a spiritual email[3]) about shame, and so he was perfectly positioned to have that conversation at that time. Had we tried to respond to the reviewers any earlier, the conversation with Uncle Max would have been different. That all things happen in their right time is a central cultural understanding and one

---

3   Spiritual emails can take many forms and in this case it was a message from Country that triggered a memory of something that was learnt previously.

that challenges Western understandings of time as linear – the ideas that underpin research 'timelines' and 'milestones':

> In an Aboriginal worldview, time to the extent that it exists at all is neither linear nor absolute. There are patterns and systems of energy that create and transform, from the ageing process of the human body to the growth and decay of the broader universe. But these processes are not 'measured' or even framed in a strictly temporal sense, and certainly not in a linear sense. (Kwaymullina & Kwaymullina, 2010, p. 199)

Uncle Max's memory and our asking questions about shame happened in a pattern and system of energy that connected them to occur in their right time, and this was respected by the authoring team. In this context, respect is easy~difficult and could be right~wrong depending on the circumstances. For example, we also must respect~challenge Western 'deadlines'. In delaying the response to the reviewers in this story, intentionally or because of prompts from patterns and systems of energy, we took a risk in the current publish-or-perish climate familiar to universities everywhere, but we also respected things happening in their own time. This respect for time in the research process was right~wrong, easy~difficult, and in looking at 'both sides of these tilde' this tripartation approach has the potential to facilitate community research in decolonising ways.

Concluding and enduring questions for 'community-led' data analysis and authorship

We had an easy answer to most difficult questions, but communicating an easy answer was difficult when you look at everything in connection. The question was easy as we could go to the community to ask the difficult question; the difficulty was if the answer did not meet Western thinking or the academy's political posturing of knowledge. 'Answers' from community sometimes can be viewed as too 'simplistic' and under-theorised to report directly as research findings. Then it becomes difficult.

Easy and difficult are intertwined, not a binary. Just going to the Aboriginal community is not easy when university protocols don't match Aboriginal protocols (and vice versa). It can also be seen as easy if you do not work with the community. But if this is the case, the difficulty comes when the research does not meet university Aboriginal ethical or consultation protocols or when the Aboriginal community notes and negatively reacts to lack of consultation and partnership. However, for the Aboriginal academic or the non-Aboriginal academic who knows the 'right' thing to do and the protocols to follow, avoiding consultation is not considered the 'easy way'; we know that starting badly ends badly. When is it right to go to the community and when is it wrong to go to the community? When is it wrong to give our academic responsibilities to the community who may or may not be getting any reciprocation? How do we describe and justify the benefits of the research? Is this reciprocation or CLR?

It is easy to ask a question but hard to know the right way to analyse the answer when you place a theory onto it. Will theory converse with story (and vice versa) and does it need to or will it stand on its own? Do we find a connection to get both a right and a wrong answer to a question that is both easy and hard to figure out? Therefore, what is the middle ground of these questions and answers, in a third space that is mobile and dynamic? Are we answering the question to please the community, or the university, or the funding body? Or, are we answering the question on how we (I) the researcher sees the answer?

So how do we navigate what is easy, difficult, right and wrong? Whilst we have no answers, we have a few driving questions that should propel us through our future research:

- How can academics do a better job of 'connecting' research interests with community interests and work? And why should/shouldn't this happen? Will researchers listen to when community want and don't want academic research?
- How can we reform the research relationship and how research questions are identified by positioning Country as the focus?
- How can academics resist researching communities and instead trust that communities already have the 'answers' to their questions? In doing this, can researchers and communities instead turn the Western academic research foci to co-investigations of the societal,

institutional and policy structures that enable and constrain communities' answers? For example, the Australian Aboriginal community already has the framework for resolving problems through stories from Country.

- How can universities learn to 'walk the talk' in resourcing high-impact, high-usefulness research for communities?
- How can academic communities (funding bodies, universities etc.) adjust expectations around the time required to work respectfully with communities?
- How can academics push and agitate the conventions of reporting brief methodology sections in academic journals so that the importance of method in community research gains 'scholarly traction'?
- How can academics challenge discourses of 'credibility' and 'impartiality' in analysis so as to involve 'community' in authentic data analysis and reporting of findings?

CLR is right, wrong, easy and difficult.

Acknowledgements

In addition to all the people who were involved in writing the 'No shame at AIME' paper (McKnight et al., 2019), we would also like to thank Dr Christine Grice and Ann Leaf for pointing us in the direction of some very helpful reading regarding distributed and shared leadership in educational contexts.

References

Archibald, J-A. (1997). *Coyote learns to make a storybasket: The place of First Nations stories in education* (Unpublished doctoral dissertation). Simon Fraser University, Burnaby. https://bit.ly/3v2eBPa.

Bush, T. (2013). Distributed leadership: The model of choice in the 21st century. *Educational Management Administration & Leadership, 41*(5), pp. 543–544.

Grice, C. (2019). Distributed pedagogical leadership for the implementation of mandated curriculum change. *Leading and Managing, 25*(1), pp. 56–71.

Harrison, M. D. & Mcconchie, P. (2009). *My people's dreaming: An Aboriginal elder speaks on life, land, spirit and forgiveness.*Warriewood, NSW: Finch Publishing.

Ireland, B. (2009). *Moving from the head to the heart: Addressing the Indian's Canada problem in reclaiming the learning spirit: Aboriginal learners in education.* Saskatoon: University of Saskatchewan, Aboriginal Education Research Centre; Calgary: First Nations and Adult Higher Education Consortium.

Kwaymullina, A. & Kwaymullina, B. (2010). Learning to read the signs: Law in an Indigenous reality. *Journal of Australian Studies, 34*(2), pp. 195–208.

Lumby, J. (2013). Distributed leadership: The uses and abuses of power. *Educational Management Administration and Leadership, 41*(5), pp. 581–597.

McHugh, T. F., Coppola, A. M., Holt, N. L. & Andersen, C. (2015). 'Sport is community': An exploration of urban Aboriginal peoples' meanings of community within the context of sport. *Psychology of Sport and Exercise, 18,* pp. 75–84.

McKnight, A. D. (2015). Mingadhuga mingayung: Respecting country through mother Mountain's stories to share her cultural voice in Western academic structures. *Educational Philosophy and Theory, 47*(3), pp. 276–290.

McKnight, A., Harwood, V., McMahon, S., Priestly, A. & Trindorfer, J. (2019). 'No shame at AIME': Listening to Aboriginal philosophy and methodologies to theorise shame in educational contexts. *The Australian Journal of Indigenous Education, 49*(1), pp. 46–56. doi:10.1017/jie.2018.14.

Rose, D. B. (1996). *Nourishing terrains: Australian Aboriginal views of landscape and wilderness.* Canberra: Australian Heritage Commission.

Rose, D. B. (2004). *Reports from a wild country: Ethics for decolonisation.* Sydney: University of New South Wales Press.

Spillane, J. P., Halverson, R. & Diamond, J. B. (2004). Towards a theory of leadership practice: A distributed perspective. *Journal of Curriculum Studies, 36*(1), pp. 3–34.

Youngs, H. (2017). A critical exploration of collaborative and distributed leadership in higher education: Developing an alternative ontology through leadership-as-practice. *Journal of Higher Education Policy and Management, 39*(2), pp. 140–154.

4
The killer boomerang and other lessons learnt on the journey to undertaking Community-Led Research

Emma Webster, Yvonne Hill, Allan Hall and Cecil See

> Your culture is not what your hands touch – it is what moves your hands. (NSW Department of Education, 2012)

This chapter is written for researchers who are interested in working alongside Aboriginal people and communities to do Community-Led Research (CLR). Whatever the reason for choosing to undertake CLR, it can be challenging to get started. In fact, this can be so challenging that it prevents you from taking any action at all. We hope to encourage you to take those first steps towards CLR by sharing our journey and some Aboriginal processes we used to engage with Aboriginal knowledge and to work with Aboriginal people.

First, we would like to introduce ourselves and acknowledge our ancestors and the Country we are from and on, as this is an Aboriginal cultural protocol. Yvonne Hill and Cecil See are proud descendants of the Wiradjuri Nation and Allan Hall is a proud descendant of the Gamilaroi and Yuwaallaraay Nations. Emma Webster is a non-Aboriginal woman

E. Webster, Y. Hill, A. Hall & C. See (2021). The killer boomerang and other lessons learnt on the journey to undertaking Community-Led Research. In V. Rawlings, J. Flexner & L. Riley (Eds.), *Community-Led Research: Walking new pathways together*. Sydney: Sydney University Press.

with Wendish, Prussian and English ancestry. Allan Hall is a Senior Aboriginal Education and Engagement Advisor with the New South Wales Education Bangamalanha Centre. Yvonne Hill and Cecil See are Aboriginal Education and Engagement Officers with the Bangamalanha Centre and Emma Webster is a research academic with the University of Sydney's School of Rural Health. We all live and work on the special Country of the Wiradjuri people and give our respect to Elders past and present. We extend that respect to you, the reader.

The chapter starts with a story from Yvonne Hill about the killer boomerang and resolving the tension or conflict which happens in learning when two ideas or perspectives contradict each other. Using the same framework from the killer boomerang story, Emma Webster will share how she came to undertake CLR and projects. We then consider integrity in CLR, exploring how axiology, ontology, epistemology and methodology differ between Aboriginal and Western approaches. We learn about the cultural interface through a story about the returning boomerang and will finish the chapter with our thoughts about what it would take for CLR to flourish in the future.

We would like to acknowledge those who have come before us and to shared their knowledge. They have inspired us to learn about CLR and share what we know with you. In the spirit of 'if you take something, put something back' (NSW Department of Education, 2019), we encourage you to share your knowledge with others in the future.

We want to be clear how we are using the term CLR. Community-led means community members have or share power over the purpose, objectives and actions undertaken in a research study or project. This does not mean that the community does all the research, but does anticipate that participatory methods are used.

The killer boomerang story

My name is Yvonne Hill. I am a Wiradjuri woman and Aboriginal Education and Engagement Officer with the New South Wales Department of Education. The killer boomerang is a useful tool and weapon and is shaped like a number seven with a long blade and a short blade. I am going to share a story about the killer boomerang and

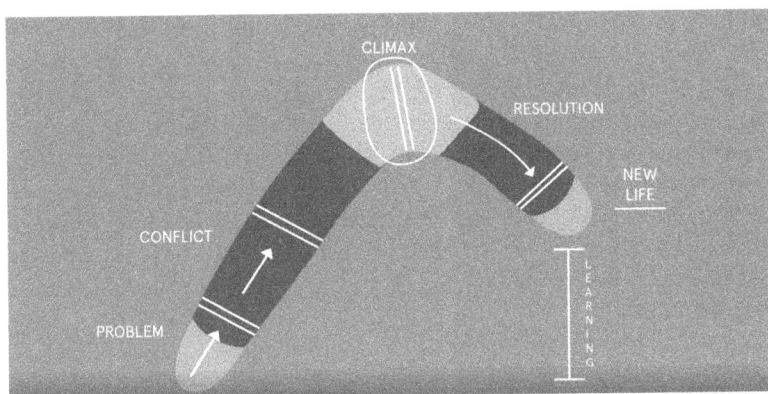

Figure 4.1 The Killer Boomerang shows how new learning comes from solving a problem. (Yvonne Hill and Cornel Ozies, 2019)

how we can use this shape to resolve tension or conflict and bring new learning and understanding. (You can find this and other stories in a resource prepared for educators: NSW Department of Education, 2012.)

At the start of any learning there is a problem or issue, something you are trying to fix, learn or try, something that we can have a conversation about. The next stage is the discord or *conflict*. You might have one idea about what is important and yet someone else has a different idea of what they think is important. Conflict gives you the opportunity to build trust through conversation. This leads to the *climax*, where both parties understand what is to be achieved. *Resolution* is what we have learnt about ourselves and the other person. Resolution leads to the *learning* or the *new life*, embedded within us forever (see Figure 4.1).

Let us think of these processes in an everyday scenario, like the Christmas Day when I receive my first bike. The *problem* is I do not know how to ride a bike. The *conflict* is that Dad thinks it is time for me to learn how to ride a bike. But I am not so sure that I want to ride a bike. There are lots of thoughts and misconceptions about what could happen ... I will not be able to learn all the skills to ride a bike and I will fall off and hurt myself! There need to be lots of conversations that happen to give reassurance when helping a child learn how to ride a bike. You need to have conversations to build trust. Within the conflict comes the opportunity to build trust. Then we come to the *climax*. There are lots of things to riding a bike. You need co-ordination, balance, to know how to steer and pedal simultaneously, and to learn how to stop. Dad says, 'By George, I think she's got it' and I know why Dad wanted me to get on the bike because this is fun and I am going to be a great bike rider. The *resolution* is the new learning and new life I can have, now I know how to ride a bike. I will never go back to not knowing how to ride a bike; that *learning* is embedded within me forever.

My journey to CLR

My name is Emma Webster. I am a non-Aboriginal woman living on Wiradjuri Country in Dubbo, western New South Wales. Until 2014 I had only undertaken research using Western approaches. Both my training and my workplace valued these 'evidence-based' approaches.

An important moment in my journey began when listening to a doctoral candidate present her thesis about decolonising research methods (Sherwood, 2010). Her argument was that the very process of doing research was of itself colonising in that the axiology (values), ontology (existence), epistemology (knowledge) and methodology (practice) were all at odds with Aboriginal peoples and culture. This was a concept I could not get out of my head as it brought to light a problem with how I had practised research.

I mentally checked the research I had been involved in previously. In contrast with Aboriginal values, I had analysed data focused only on identifying deficits (Jeuken & Douglas, 1997). I had undertaken research where Aboriginal people were absent from any consideration, but in hindsight could have benefited from the research (Fitzgerald, Bunde-Birouste & Webster, 2009; Liddle et al., 2008; Liddle et al., 2007; Malek, McLean & Webster, 2007; Webster, Thomas, Ong & Cutler, 2011). While I had discussions with Aboriginal Elders and community members, this was rarely focused on building relationships as a foundation for research collaboration. Also rare was any evidence of influence on methodology or methods from either discussion with Aboriginal people or published literature on Indigenous approaches.

Not to excuse my own actions, I also recognised the influence of working in a professional discipline (public health and medicine) where historically we have done things *for* people and *to* people rather than *with* people (Rawlings & McDermott, this volume; Riley, this volume). Similarly, my employers had also privileged Western empirical knowledge and ways of operating over Indigenous knowledges and Indigenous ways of operating (Welsh & Burgess, this volume). These beliefs have led to health services and research actions undertaken in the name of public health and medicine which have had detrimental effects for Aboriginal people (Riley, this volume). A local example of public health action from the late 1960s was the forced moving of Aboriginal families from government reserves to live in town. The government reserve was located on traditional homelands about ten kilometres from town. Healthy cultural foods (such as kangaroo, emu and fish) were present in abundance and strong social and cultural connections existed between family groups. Living in town provided housing with sanitation and came with the instant burden of owing money for rent, no access to healthy food, and loss of social capital and spiritual connection to the land. An example from medicine is the primacy of Western birthing practices (requiring all women to birth in a hospital where anaesthetists, obstetricians and gynaecologists are available) imposed on Aboriginal women, forcing them to birth away from traditional homelands and in the absence of culturally significant practices.

These reflections led me to consider the following questions. How might I have approached and done research differently? How would this have influenced the results? Would the Aboriginal community have been better served if research was done this way? Would the findings have resulted in more useful outcomes? Would the results have been as influential within the organisation? I felt this conflict or tension about my own research, and I started to observe the same discord when I read and heard about the research others were doing. I wondered if it were possible, as a non-Aboriginal researcher, to undertake Indigenous-focused research and by applying decolonising methods to meet the requirements of both Aboriginal communities and my employers.

An opportunity arose to work with Aboriginal colleagues on a research study prescribed by our organisations. I could bring expertise on the Western way to do research, but needed conversations with those who have cultural knowledge to challenge the usual way to proceed and how to interpret data. Asking Aboriginal co-researchers 'Who else should we be talking to?' invited new voices to the conversation and privileged cultural knowledge. When cultural advice challenges the methodological approach you usually take, this is exactly the moment where your deliberate decisions act to disrupt the Western paradigm and decolonise your research (Riley, this volume). These are the moments of conflict which build trust. These conversations brought us to a common understanding or climax and the resolution was to approach research in a new way. Details about the research have been reported elsewhere (Webster, Johnson, Kemp et al., 2017) as have the specific tensions between Western and Aboriginal approaches that arose in applying a decolonising lens (Webster, Johnson, Johnson et al., 2017).

The research resulted in the usual contributions to academia such as conference papers and publications. In addition, co-researcher Aboriginal health practitioners developed research skills which helped later evaluation of projects in their broader work team. I consider these *results*, as they were expected, rather than *new learning*, which was unexpected.

The new learning for me included seeing how much participants enjoyed the focus groups. So much so that this led to the establishment of a monthly Aboriginal chronic disease support group. I had run many focus groups previously, but never one that people wanted to come to every month! The chronic disease support group strengthened long-term social relationships and provided a safe place for community and clinicians to come together to learn from each other. Keeping Aboriginal community leaders informed on the progress of the research kept the focus on community benefits. When sharing what I thought would be our final progress report, these leaders told us this was just the beginning and provided instruction as to the topic and the nature of the next piece of work, including volunteers to assist. This was when the relationship changed to *community-led*. While this had not been the original intention, sufficient trust had been established by applying decolonising methodology to change the relationship and give the community confidence that there was tangible benefit in research and that their values were respected and their voice was heard. A subsequent project prepared a teaching resource for students studying medicine, nursing and health sciences to learn how to yarn (a communication style which privileges Aboriginal processes) to enhance future communication in healthcare settings. Medical students now host the Aboriginal community annually for a meal around the campfire to build relationships and yarn. Aboriginal community members also regularly suggest guest speakers, share cultural knowledge in tutorials or invite students to community events as a direct result of this community-led approach.

This is my new journey, or *new life*, embedded within me forever. I still apply Western research approaches, but I prefer to look for opportunities to apply decolonising methodology and respond to community suggestions which facilitate CLR and projects.

Axiology, ontology, epistemology and methodology … does it matter which comes first?

We all hold certain values and beliefs. This is not obvious to us when all the people we know and deal with hold the same values and beliefs. But when these differ, whether it is in education or health or research, there is a dissonance that can be difficult to reconcile.

When preparing a research project in the Western tradition we would usually start with intellectual processes (shown in Figure 4.2). We would start by defining the research question, considering what others who have studied this topic have found and what the 'gap' in the knowledge is. We would then follow this with operational processes. How can we find out the answer? What data needs to be collected? How do we collect it? What methods are needed to analyse the data? Once we have thoroughly thought through our research, we then consider the ethical implications and whether what we are planning to study meets the values of our society. When the research is complete, we consider how the research might be translated to others to change their knowledge or influence the way they work (relational processes).

The order of our progress prioritises these intellectual and operational processes over the ethical and relational processes. This has a profound influence on how research is conceptualised and undertaken.

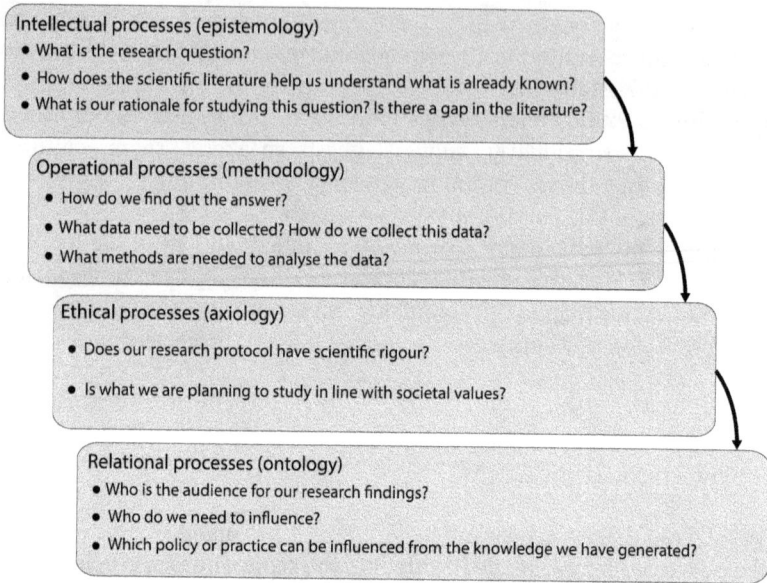

Figure 4.2 A Western approach to designing and undertaking research.

Taking an Aboriginal approach to designing and undertaking research would start with consideration of ethical and relational processes first (shown in Figure 4.3). We would start by learning about local cultural protocols we need to follow to undertake the research in a way that is consistent with a specific community's values and beliefs. We would consider how the Aboriginal community would benefit from this research. Questions to follow this would include: Who should we be talking to? How will decisions be made? What will our responsibilities be as knowledge holders at the completion of the research? Which conversations do we need to have? We would then consider the research question and operational processes relating to what will constitute data and how we will analyse and interpret this data. These questions might include: Who is the keeper of the knowledge we should study? What counts as knowledge? What is our research question? What will constitute data? Who will analyse the data and how will data be interpreted? Placing ethical and relational processes ahead of

Ethical processes (axiology)
- What is the cultural protocol we must follow for this community?
- How will the community benefit from this research?
- What will our responsibilities be as knowledge holders?

Relational processes (ontology)
- Who should we be talking to?
- How will decisions be made?
- What conversations do we need to have?

Intellectual processes (epistemology)
- What counts as knowledge?
- Who is the keeper of the knowledge we want to study?
- What is our research question?

Operational processes (methodology)
- What will constitute data?
- Who will analyse the data?
- How will data be interpreted?

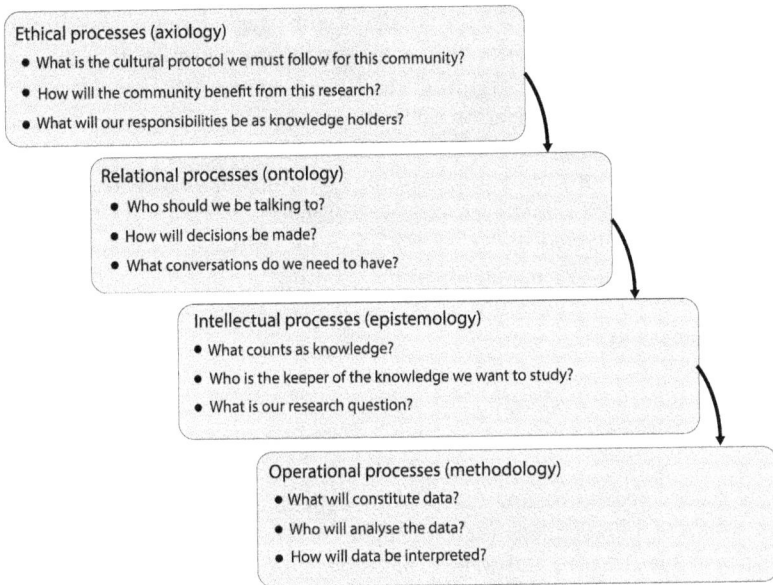

Figure 4.3 An Aboriginal approach to designing and undertaking research

intellectual and operational processes *orientates* the researcher to values and beliefs of the community and ensures these shape and plan the subsequent research.

We can see in these examples just how different the same research conducted by the same research team might be if the processes are re-ordered. It is also much clearer to see how the very process of doing research can be colonising, even when undertaken by well-meaning and well-trained researchers. If we come back to the need for community to have or share power in setting research priorities and undertaking CLR, placing ethical and relational processes ahead of intellectual and operational processes provides a practical framework to apply Aboriginal processes when working with Aboriginal people.

Considering Aboriginal processes to engage with Aboriginal knowledges and guide work with Aboriginal people is documented in *8 ways Aboriginal pedagogy* (NSW Department of Education, 2019; NSW Department of Education, 2012; Yunkaporta, 2009). There are also many excellent guides that detail the steps researchers should undertake in their work with Aboriginal communities to produce meaningful research (Gwynn et al., 2015; Laycock, Walker, Harrison & Brands, 2009, 2011; National Health and Medical Research Council, 2018a, 2018b; Riley, this volume; Welsh & Burgess, this volume). All outline the importance of building relationships and trust with communities prior to developing research questions or undertaking research. The development of relationships between academics and communities takes time and genuine commitment, and is not without risk to both parties as funding of proposed research is never guaranteed (Robinson et al., this volume).

The returning boomerang and the cultural interface

The returning boomerang can provide us with a way to see the process of different perspectives coming together. The returning boomerang has two blades of equal length. Returning boomerangs are specially flighted to ensure that when they are thrown correctly, they return to the thrower. Returning to the thrower is their specific purpose. To reach the apex of the returning boomerang, you must travel exactly the same distance along each blade. The metaphor of throwing the boomerang and having it return to you could also relate to throwing respect or goodness out and having it come back to you.

We will use the returning boomerang shape to represent when two perspectives are very different, and where there is low knowledge from the holders of each perspective (see Figure 4.4). In our case, the ends of each blade are Aboriginal and Western perspectives on research and the distance between these ends represents the difference or 'gap' between these perspectives. To learn about the other perspective, we first must start with a conversation. If we do not have a conversation we will never get to the next level of understanding. Each conversation increases our knowledge of the alternative perspective and takes us a step closer to the apex. As our knowledge of Aboriginal and Western perspectives increases over many conversations, a relationship is built. Further conversations build on the relationship and it becomes a partnership (NSW Department of Education, 2012). The apex of the

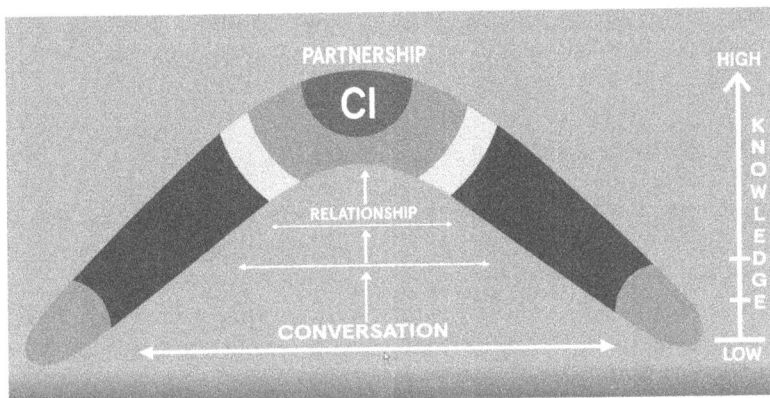

Figure 4.4 The returning boomerang showing the cultural interface (Yvonne Hill and Cornel Ozies, 2019).

boomerang is where Aboriginal and Western knowledges come together in what Nakata would describe as the cultural interface (Nakata, 2007). This is a contested space, neither Aboriginal nor Western. This is the place where true, honest, purposeful partnerships exist, where different systems of knowledge find common ground and where innovation can occur. If we do not achieve that honest, purposeful partnership, then we are not in it for the long run and we are not going to be successful.

Using the metaphor or story of the returning boomerang helps prioritise ethical and relational processes by encouraging conversations to increase knowledge of each other's perspective. The work of sharing and listening must be done equally by each party to keep balance in the returning boomerang. Both sides must remain equal so that the returning boomerang delivers on the specific purpose of the partnership.

When you are explicit about your values and beliefs you can make deliberate decisions about how you will proceed with your research by defining what is important. Sometimes this will be to privilege one approach over another (privilege an Aboriginal approach over a Western one or vice versa), or you might try a pluralist approach where you bring the 'two worlds' together at the cultural interface. If you are not explicit about your values and beliefs, these decisions are still made, but they are largely unconscious and hide the perspective you are privileging.

What is needed for CLR to really flourish?

We would like to conclude this chapter with a vision for the future of CLR. We imagine Aboriginal communities initiating contact and working in partnership with Aboriginal and non-Aboriginal researchers at the cultural interface. Aboriginal communities and researchers would be supported by a grant system which funded their research in two stages.

The first stage would fund ethical and relational processes and would not be limited to a topic (such as cancer or dementia) and would allow time to assemble the right team of community members and researchers to build relationships and determine a mutually agreed direction for research (Welsh & Burgess, this volume). The funding parameters would ensure community members and Elders were remunerated for their cultural knowledge in a way that fairly represented their expertise and experience (see Flexner, this volume, for discussion of the limits of research to be decolonised when wealth differentials are not properly regarded). Likewise, data sovereignty, intellectual property and copyright would be negotiated in a way that is fair to all parties.

The second stage of the grant would look more like the grants we are familiar with, except co-design principles underpin the building of research questions, data collection instruments and data collection (Rawlings & McDermott, this volume) and collective analysis and interpretation (McMahon & McKnight, this volume).

Progress reports to funders would be done in person, with Aboriginal and non-Aboriginal representatives from the funding body coming to visit the community-led team to hear about the conversations they have had and the mutual learning that has taken place. Dissemination would be funded to include hosting other Aboriginal communities and researchers to share both the process and the outcomes of the research. Research impact would be measured by the community benefits of the research alongside benefits to individual researchers. A further measure of research impact might be community recommendation of researchers to other communities.

Grant applications for CLR would start with a joint verbal expression of interest by community and researchers to the fund holder resulting in some applicants being invited to submit a written application. The assessment panel would consist of Aboriginal community members and Aboriginal and non-Aboriginal researchers, and would prioritise applications based on the confidence that ethical and relational processes would be followed to establish true, honest, purposeful partnerships. Then CLR would really flourish!

A non-Aboriginal voice as co-author of a chapter on Aboriginal perspectives

As a non-Aboriginal woman, it follows accepted protocol for me to explain how I have come to co-author a chapter on Aboriginal perspectives and processes for community leadership in research. My voice is important in this story because there are other non-Aboriginal people who would like to be more effective in ensuring fairer health and education outcomes for First Nations people … and I hope there always will be. Sometimes non-Aboriginal people do not know how to start, or proceed, or are concerned that any mistake they make will make the situation worse. Hearing about my journey is intended as encouragement. It shows *a* way (not *the* way) that relationships can be built and good quality research can be done in true partnership with Aboriginal people. You are encouraged to make your *own* journey.

I have benefitted from walking alongside my Aboriginal friends and colleagues, learning new and collaborative ways of doing research. As my own journey continues, I am working on identifying my own values and beliefs and learning more about ethical and relational processes. One of those ethical processes is relational responsibility. As I hold knowledge of CLR, I now have a responsibility to share this knowledge with others. Contributing to this chapter has provided one avenue to fulfil this responsibility.

Conclusion

In this chapter you have been introduced to Aboriginal processes and how following these processes brings integrity to CLR. Undertaking ethical and relational processes first acts as an orientation to the community and must be embarked upon before intellectual or operational processes of research occur. The returning boomerang provides a framework to start the conversations that build meaningful, purposeful partnerships. Following these cultural protocols positions you to share, learn and create contested space at the cultural interface for new understandings to be generated. The contested space can be a place of tension or conflict, occurring when you challenge your own values, beliefs, knowledges and practices when learning the perspectives of others. The killer boomerang story shows that trust is built through conflict and that learning is not just bringing new facts to light, but a new way of doing things and a new life. Stepping out of your usual way of practising research might create conflict, but it is also creating an opportunity to build trust and improve the quality of research.

References

Fitzgerald, E., Bunde-Birouste. A. & Webster, E. (2009). Through the eyes of children: Engaging primary school-aged children in creating supportive school enviornments for physical activity and nutrition. *Health Promotion Journal of Australia, 20*(2), pp. 127–132. doi: 10.1071/he09127.

Gwynn, J., Lock, M., Turner, N., Dennison, R., Coleman, C., Kelly, B. & Wiggers, J. (2015). Aboriginal and Torres Strait Islander community governance of health research: Turning principles into practice. *Australian Journal of Rural Health, 23*(4), pp. 235–242. doi:10.1111/ajr.12182.

Jeuken, M. & Douglas, M. (Eds.) (1997). *A picture of health: The health status of the people of the Macquarie Area.* East Dubo, NSW: Centre for Population Health, Macquarie Helath Service.

Laycock, A., Walker, D., Harrison, N. & Brands, J. (2009). *Supporting Indigenous researchers: A practical guide for supervisors.* Casuarina, NT: Cooperative Research Centre for Aboriginal Health. http://bit.ly/2OuRTi3.

Laycock, A., Walker, D., Harrison, N. & Brands, J. (2011). *Researching Indigenous health: A practical guide for researchers*. Carton South, VIC: The Lowitja Institute. http://bit.ly/30pqTmJ.

Liddle, J., Jones, T., Lesjak, M., Milat, A., Lyle, D. & Webster, E. (2008). Influencing population health performance: Feedback from managers, population health staff and clinicians on the NSW Population Health Standards for Area Health Services. *NSW Public Health Bulletin, 19*(7–8), pp. 117–120. doi: 10.1071/nb07001.

Liddle, J., Lyle, D., Lesjack, M., Milat, A., Webster, E. & Jones, T. (2007). Influencing population health performance: introduction of standards for Area Health Services in NSW. *NSW Public Health Bulletin, 18*(1–2), pp. 1–5. doi: 10.1071/nb07016.

Malek, S., McLean, R. & Webster, E. (2007). Analysis of recording and coding of smoking history for patients admitted to a regional hospital. *Australian Journal of Rural Health, 15*(1), pp. 65–66.

Nakata, M. (2007). The cultural interface. *Australian Journal of Indigenous Education, 36*, pp. 7–14.

National Health and Medical Research Council (2018a). *Ethical conduct in research with Aboriginal and Torres Strait Islander peoples and communities: Guidelines for researchers and stakeholders*. http://bit.ly/2MUVnK6.

National Health and Medical Research Council (2018b). *Keeping research on track II. A companion document to ethical conduct in research with Aboriginal and Torres Strait Islander peoples and communities: Guidelines for researchers and stakeholders*. http://bit.ly/38jFQuG.

NSW Department of Education (2019). *8 ways Aboriginal pedagogy*. https://www.8ways.online/about.

NSW Department of Education (2012). *8 ways: Aboriginal pedagogy from Western NSW*. Sydney: NSW Department of Education and Training.

Sherwood, J. (2010). *Do no harm: Decolonising Aboriginal health research* (Doctoral dissertation). University of NSW, Sydney.

Webster, E., Johnson, C., Johnson, M., Kemp, B., Smith, V. & Townsend, B. (2017). Engaging Aboriginal people in research: Taking a decolonizing gaze. In P. Liamputtong (Ed.), *Handbook of research methods in health social sciences*, pp. 1563–78. Singapore: Springer.

Webster, E., Johnson, C., Kemp, B., Smith, V., Johnson, M. & Townsend, B. (2017). Theory that explains an Aboriginal perspective of learning to understand and manage diabetes. *Australian and New Zealand Journal of Public Health, 41*(1), pp. 27–31. doi: 10.1111/1753-6405.12605.

Webster, E., Thomas, M., Ong, N. & Cutler, L. (2011). Rural research capacity building program: Capacity building outcomes. *Australian Journal of Primary Health, 17*(7). doi: 10.1071/PY10060 1448–7527/11/010107.

Yunkaporta, T. (2009). *Aboriginal pedagogies at the cultural interface* (Doctoral dissertation). James Cook University, Townsville. http://eprints.jcu.edu.au/ 10974

5

What is a researcher? Definitions, bureaucracy and ironies in the Australian context

Helena Robinson, James L. Flexner and Imelda Miller

research
/rəˈsɜtʃ/ (say ruh'serch),
/ˈrisɜtʃ/ (say 'reeserch)
noun 1. diligent and systematic inquiry or investigation into a subject in order to discover facts or principles. (Macquarie Dictionary 2003)
researcher

1. A person who researches; an investigator, inquirer.
2. A person employed to undertake research, esp. in an academic or scientific institution. (Oxford English Dictionary, 2019)

In 2016, a team of academics from the University of Sydney and the University of Queensland, together with curatorial staff from the Queensland Museum, began drafting a research project to investigate

H. Robinson, J.L. Flexner & I. Miller (2021). What is a researcher? Definitions, bureaucracy and ironies in the Australian context. In V. Rawlings, J. Flexner & L. Riley (Eds.), *Community-Led Research: Walking new pathways together*. Sydney: Sydney University Press.

the heritage of Australian South Sea Islanders in full co-operation with the stakeholder communities. Led by James Flexner, the team held preparatory meetings with Australian South Sea Islander groups to test the feasibility of the project, to develop project aims that reflected their cultural, social and political aspirations, and to draft a methodological approach fully integrating Australian South Sea Islanders as research experts and partners.

Conceived within the decolonising model of maximal participatory research (Gonzalez, Kretzler & Edwards, 2018), early drafts of the funding proposal identified Australian South Sea Islander community groups as partner institutions and outlined a flexible methodological framework to include research approaches and outcomes authentic to the stakeholders. Over the course of its development, however, the research grant document transformed in response to the requirements of the Australian Research Council (ARC) and its Linkage Projects scheme. Responding to the ARC's funding rules and research advisers' feedback on the eligibility of our application, successive iterations of the draft proposal saw the participatory role of Australian South Sea Islanders in the project downplayed. Only the researchers with formal academic qualifications or roles at the Queensland Museum were listed as Chief or Partner Investigators (CIs and PIs), while the methodological outline for the project became focused on conventional, academically recognised approaches and outputs.

Using our experience of writing the ARC funding application, this chapter explores the tension between scholarship that aspires towards a culturally democratic, shared-authority research model and existing funding frameworks still tethered to hierarchical notions of research expertise. By analysing documents and correspondence generated in the development of the research grant application, this chapter provides a rich description of the grant application writing process, including analysis of the sequence of decision-making that underpinned the transformation of the project from its initial objectives into its final submitted form.

To be clear, we are not singling out the ARC specifically in this chapter. The problems we encountered in framing the funding application for this particular project resonate far outside of the

Australian context. Despite decades of calls for 'decolonising' research (Tuhiwai Smith, 2012), there are still tensions between the limiting structures of the academic research environment and the ideals of a community-led paradigm. The ARC has a history of funding community-oriented archaeological research, particularly involving Aboriginal groups (e.g. Veth et al., 2019),[1] but a narrow understanding of researcher expertise persists in the structural and discursive norms of funding proposals.

This chapter was written at the commencement of the research project, which gained ARC funding approval in 2018. It is divided into sections that document each phase in the development of the grant application. As part of our commitment to reflexive practice, our narrative captures a snapshot of the temporal, methodological, political and institutional challenges of merging academic research with community expectations and the implications that these challenges may pose for the life cycle of the project.

First draft

> We seek to ensure that all plans are in the interest of the community ... How can we do that if we are not involved from the beginning? (Mackay and District Australian South Sea Islander Association, 2000, p. 23)

In 2000, Queensland Premier Peter Beattie's preamble to his government's *Action Plan for Australian South Sea Islanders* called for special consideration of the needs and goals of the Australian South Sea Islander community, based on a history of unequal opportunity and lack of recognition (Queensland Government, 2000). The ability of the community to participate fully in the cultural life of Queensland was seen as integral to the Action Plan, reflecting the interconnectivity between cultural self-expression and broader economic, political and

---

1   The related ARC grant was titled Murujuga – Dynamics of the Dreaming (2014–16), administered by the University of Western Australia. For details see https://bit.ly/30kUihE.

social participation. As expressed in the plan, the Queensland government's desire to support Australian South Sea Islander culture and identity was instrumental to the extent that it regarded improved understanding of the community's cultural needs as a pathway to tailoring the delivery of government services, building capacity within the community and highlighting significant Australian South Sea Islander contributions to Queensland's economic and social development. To some extent the plan was also a conciliatory gesture in recognition of the role played by historical legislation in formalising discrimination against the community, and subsequent legacies of disadvantage (Beattie, Hollis & Borbidge, 2000).

Within this political context, part of the rationale for our project was to galvanise official efforts to redress Australian South Sea Islander experiences of systemic inequality (including those historically caused by the actions of government bodies) by challenging conventional, academic-led notions of research. We wanted to develop and trial a new model for research founded on the principles of genuine participation and self-determination on the part of the community. From the outset, we recognised the irony (and potential) of developing such a model within the framework of the ARC's Linkage Projects Scheme, with the opportunity to enact change from within a prescriptively academic and institutionally focused program.

The idea for a collaborative project on Australian South Sea Islander heritage through the lens of archaeology and museum collections first came up in 2014 when James Flexner travelled to Brisbane to undertake a study of New Hebrides (Vanuatu) objects in the Queensland Museum (QM) collection in connection with his ongoing archaeological investigations in the Vanuatu region. During this trip, Flexner met Geraldine Mate and Imelda Miller, both from the curatorial department at QM, and they began discussing what kind of project might be possible.

Australian South Sea Islander communities have long worked on their own projects in historical research and community development, not least in connection to the official recognition of Australian South Sea Islanders by the Queensland government in 1994 and the commemorations that accompanied the 150th anniversary of the first arrival of South Sea Islander labourers in Queensland in 2013. Both the recognition and the 150th anniversary were watershed events in which the QM, and specifically Miller, were intimately involved. There was a sense that in spite of these incremental steps, more could be done to explore and educate the public about Australian South Sea Islander pasts in relation to lived identities. The development of such a project was not just intellectually engaging, but of personal interest to Miller, who is of Australian South Sea Islander background.

In 2016, Mate, Miller and Flexner revisited the idea of applying for ARC funding for the project. Supported by funding from the University of Sydney and QM, a preliminary meeting was held at QM Southbank, followed by an initial field trip to Mackay, Ayr, Rockhampton and Joskeleigh to examine promising sites and meet with community organisations. During this trip, Flexner and Mate were introduced to Australian South Sea Islander organisations including the Mackay and District Australian South Sea Islander Association (MADASSIA) and the Rockhampton Area South Sea Islander Association (RASSIC).

Following the initial field visits, a workshop was hosted at QM Southbank in November 2016. It was attended by a number of Australian South Sea Islander community leaders, as well as researchers and representatives of potential partner organisations. The first day of the workshop focused on identifying the community's research priorities, while the second day was centred on research development from an academic and institutional perspective. Also joining the team during this workshop were Thomas Baumgartl, an environmental scientist, and Andrew Fairbairn, an archaeobotanist, who could expand the scientific capacity of the project as it related to reconstructing past environments in central Queensland. Jonathan Pragnell was also brought into the team as the leading expert in the historical archaeology of Queensland (e.g. Prangnell, 2013). Representatives from the State Library of Queensland expressed their interest in being involved in the project at this point, particularly in relation to their immense and varied collections of documentary sources relating to Australian South Sea Islander history. Following the workshop, Mate and Miller returned to central Queensland to gain further direction and feedback from stakeholder groups. The Australian South Sea Islander community was very excited and looked forward to the possibilities of moving towards a full funding proposal.

Developing the application

> We do not want you to study us, we want you to work with us
> (Mackay and District Australian South Sea Islander Association,
> 2000, 19)

A community-led approach to cultural research aims not only to recover and disseminate the heritage of specific groups, but also to build skills for sustaining research activity in the community by offering community members experience in scholarly research methods. This means that Community-Led Research (CLR) does not stop at extensive community consultation, but also remains fundamentally committed to a shared research experience. In our case – and similar to initiatives that have been trialled in the context of capacity building around Aboriginal and Torres Strait Islander heritage management (Smith & Jackson, 2006; NSW Government, 2010; Greer, 2010) – we envisaged Australian South Sea Islander communities becoming more self-reliant in the practice of cultural heritage research as one of the key outcomes of our project.

The ideal of co-produced and co-managed research is not new, but there has been a lag between conceptualising changes to practice and converting that intent into tangible modifications to actual research processes. Our project began with what we hoped were the right intentions, but as we moved from the scoping stage towards translating our initial conversations with the Australian South Sea Islander community into a formal ARC Linkage application, we sensed the pressure to move away from an expressly community-led articulation of the project.

The wording of a 2016 draft of the ARC application reveals that, from the outset, the research team was conscious of the tensions between the demands of conventional scholarly research design and process – which usually includes the articulation of a research philosophy, a research question and listed aims for the study, followed by an account of recognised strategies for data collection and analysis – and the need to defer methodological closure so that the Australian South Sea Islander community could fully participate in the development of the project. The team was likewise aware that it would be contradictory to the community-led aspirations of the research to predetermine and limit its outcomes to conventional scholarly outputs that might have little relevance or direct benefit to the Australian South Sea Islander community:

> There is a degree of risk involved with this kind of collaboration, as it involves a serious investment of time and resources into activities that are often considered non-academic in nature, and sometimes results in conflicting discussions about what communities want, and how they want to be involved in research. However, we see the benefits both to the research process and the ultimate outcomes as making this risk worthwhile. (Flexner, Miller & Mate, 2016, p. 1)

The potential 'messiness' of CLR as an emergent process of collaboration and negotiation between communities and researchers over time does not, however, sit easily with bureaucratic and, arguably, conservative ARC specifications for Linkage Project applications, nor the advice we received from research advisers at the University of Sydney about how to make our proposal more competitive.

According to the ARC's 2016 Linkage Program funding rules (section A4.1.3), the purpose of the scheme is to 'deliver outcomes of benefit to Australia and build Australia's research and innovation capacity' (ARC, 2016a, p. 11). As a program that is taxpayer funded through the Australian government, the scheme justifiably emphasises the desirability of nationally accessible, useful and high-profile research outcomes that 'meet the needs of the broader Australian innovation system' (ARC, 2016a, p. 44). However, for community-led projects (where the benefits of the research logically flow to local and often minority populations) we quickly became aware that the funding application would need to emphasise more widespread return on investment within the rubric of universally recognised, predetermined scholarly methods and definitive outputs. Offering feedback on a draft of the Approach section of our proposal, one faculty research adviser wrote:

> The details are a little scant – especially for an expert assessor – experts (but non-experts too) need to get their teeth into exactly

what you're going to do, how, by whom and how long it will take.
(anon., personal communication, 2017)

Another adviser suggested that the methodological rigour of the project needed to be reinforced in terms of established fields of study, asking us to think first in disciplinary terms and restructure the methodology around 'finding new ways for ethnographic collections and field archaeology to talk to one another' (Robinson, 2017c). Ironically, on the basis of Australian South Sea Islander community organisations' limited research track record (in the context of recognised scholarly research outputs), we were questioned on the capability of the community to contribute to the development of a best-practice participatory research model (one of our stated objectives for the project). Advisers pre-empted likely questions from ARC assessors by asking: 'What would Australian South Sea Islanders actually *do* as research partners? What research expertise do Australian South Sea Islander organisations bring to the project?' (Robinson, 2017c).

In pursuit of efficient and low-risk spending of funding money, the ARC Linkage Program is geared towards facilitating collaborations between universities and non-higher education organisations that have 'demonstrated a clear commitment to high-quality research' (ARC, 2016a, p. 44). This prerequisite diminishes the possibility of nominating community organisations as partner institutions in a proposal, not least because communities are not routinely involved in research officially recognised as 'high quality' or 'high impact'. Small community organisations have limited capacity to provide material resources (either in-kind or cash) to a project, as required by the ARC. Neither can they easily muster the resources to 'enter into arrangements regarding Intellectual Property' related to a project, or necessarily elaborate how the project 'fits into each Partner Organisation's overall strategic plan' (ARC, 2016a, p. 15). These requirements preclude volunteer-run organisations like MADASSIA – our primary contact with Australian South Sea Islander people – from substantive nomination on ARC Linkage projects. As a result, we found our aspiration to cement the role of Australian South Sea Islander groups in the articulation of the project curtailed, with the University of Sydney,

University of Queensland and Queensland Museum emerging as the official research partners according to the ARC's eligibility criteria.

Final submission

> ASSIs [Australian South Sea Islanders] are not indigenous to Australia, but they have retained a singular and vibrant indigenous culture for more than 150 years of life on the Australian mainland. (Flexner et al., 2017)

In our final ARC application, we proposed an interdisciplinary and collaborative approach that would integrate the methodologies of archaeology, museology, critical heritage studies, and environmental sciences. But the methodology had to be outlined according to particular scholarly standards and narrative tropes to satisfy the ARC's assessors. As a result, the final proposal was less flexible than what had been articulated in our initial drafts. Of course, we retained some capacity to transform our approaches as we go, and indeed we expanded that ability by adding a Chief Investigator from the Australian South Sea Islander community, Francis Bobongie, with a background in education. Nonetheless, the final wording of the proposal did not go as far with the idea of a Community-Led methodology as we had initially thought possible.

The result is a project proposal that sits somewhat uncomfortably with our initial ideals for a community-led approach, but which was satisfying to the bureaucratic organisations that provide research funding in this context. Some of the proposal reflects widely accepted methodologies from the respective fields of the researchers involved. In other cases, we were able to make some recommendations in line with community desires. For example, in the realm of 'capacity building', the project will fund Research Assistant positions, with preference to recruitment of Australian South Sea Islanders. However, as the community continues to be underrepresented in higher education, it is possible there will be no suitable candidates. For example, the University of the Sunshine Coast (USC) offers a scholarship specifically for Australian South Sea Islander students, but only one, limited to $5000, is offered annually.[2]

Underpinning many of the complexities in developing our proposal is the problem of cultural recognition for Australian South Sea Islanders. Indeed, questions of recognition and respect are likely motivators for the generally sceptical stance towards outside researchers taken by many Australian South Sea Islander groups and individuals. The legislative framework in Australia, at state as well as federal level, to some degree feeds into this dynamic as it separates Aboriginal heritage from colonial (usually meaning European) heritage (see Brown, 2008). This produces a tension. On the one hand, it appropriately provides Aboriginal people with the opportunity to point to their special relationship to Country. On the other hand, it creates a wall around Aboriginal heritage that sits out of step with more recent experience; for example, with Aboriginal sites dating to the colonial period (e.g. Byrne, 2003; Harrison, 2004), or with the multicultural communities that included Aboriginal people, such as those who lived in mixed communities with Australian South Sea Islanders.

Within the context of our project, what happens with minority groups, such as Australian South Sea Islanders, who identify as 'Indigenous' but do not have the same kind of recognition as Aboriginal and Torres Strait Islander groups? Archaeologists have frameworks for working with Traditional Owners through Aboriginal corporations and Local Area Land Councils, and there are established ways of articulating these relationships, including in research grant proposals. There are established standards and protocols, and sometimes long histories of archaeologists working alongside particular Aboriginal groups who see the value of having systematic documentation of historical and ancestral ties to Country, dating back millennia.

Organisations like MADASSIA are insistent about the need to document and manage a distinctive *Australian South Sea Islander* heritage, while community members with Australian South Sea Islander and Aboriginal ancestry may apply a broader context to understanding local sites. Australian South Sea Islanders often lived alongside and sometimes intermarried with Aboriginal people,

---

2   See USC website: https://bit.ly/2MUPtIW.

particularly after the exclusionary White Australia Policy forced them off the plantations in 1908 and people moved to marginal areas along riverbanks and in the valleys. Interpreting these sites exclusively in one way or another would thus be disingenuous, even if it is somewhat at odds with the desire of some segments of the 'community' (which, of course, is far from a singular entity). Again, the labelling of sites as Aboriginal or not is a problematic legacy of interpretation, practice and legislation in Australian archaeology. In our project, we had to be sensitive about how the final submission articulated the specificity of Australian South Sea Islander focus in the project, without excluding or marginalising the related Aboriginal heritage values.

These challenges in collaborative research speak to the broader environment of cultural recognition in Australia. Models used in archaeological research, as well as other fields, to work with Aboriginal people cannot simply be translated into an Australian South Sea Islander context. Groups such as MADASSIA (2000) have their own protocols for collaborating with researchers. As our project evolves, there is an imperative to honour these guidelines as well as to forge new ways of working not envisaged within previous protocols, including in our research grant proposal, necessitating a constant process of engagement and negotiation as a new, joint methodology emerges.

The point here is not to bemoan the imperfect nature of doing collaborative research, nor to complain about the grant funding system or the politics of recognition. These are all things that are changing, and can be pushed to some extent, but they remain limiting structures we must work within to do our research at all. Rather, these limits require discussion in order to determine how future research might be shaped in order to move towards a truly community-led environment. Making the strictures of ARC definitions of researcher more flexible and better recognising and accounting for contributions from community groups would be steps in that direction.

The bigger picture: reflecting on the international context and our motivations for CLR

As a project designed to explore Australian South Sea Islander lived identities via shared authority between academics and community members, our research is nested within international heritage discourses that have been undergoing a process of transformation as the significant role of Indigenous communities in heritage management has gained prominence. The United Nation's 2007 Declaration on the Rights of Indigenous Peoples galvanised international commitments to Indigenous autonomy, affirming that Indigenous groups should not only be 'free from discrimination', but also emphasising the link between Indigenous cultures, rights and development as a subset of the right of all peoples to self-determination (UN, 2007, pp. 3–5). Explicitly linking cultural continuity with heritage practice, Article 11.1 states:

> Indigenous peoples have the right to practise and revitalize their cultural traditions and customs. This includes the right to maintain, protect and develop the past, present and future manifestations of their cultures, such as archaeological and historical sites, artefacts, designs, ceremonies, technologies and visual and performing arts and literature. (UN, 2007, pp. 11)

The 2007 Declaration shone a spotlight on issues of data sovereignty for Indigenous peoples, including their participation in gathering, and control of, research data relating to their communities (Kukutai & Taylor, 2016, pp. xxi–xxii). The need to reorientate research to serve the development agendas of Indigenous peoples, rather than solely fulfilling government requirements, has adjacent implications for scholarly research. For our project, this will mean continuous reflexive assessment of our work to ensure that there is no 'implementation gap' between the intent and realisation of community as leaders and autonomous actors in the research process. The inability to fulfil in a more complete way the ideals proposed by the Declaration on the Rights of Indigenous Peoples remains an international struggle, including within the very organisation that made the Declaration (Meskell, 2013), thus we do not take these challenges lightly.

In crafting our ARC application, we already experienced a disjuncture between authorised research discourses and the intent of a community-led approach. Early drafts of the funding application underscored the centrality of a collaborative research approach in achieving the dual purposes of the project: strengthening Australian South Sea Islander identity and contributing new scholarly knowledge through museum collection research and archaeological investigations. Even though the team was, at this stage, referring to 'community-based' rather than CLR (Flexner, Miller & Mate, 2016, p. 1), the project aims were firmly embedded in a commitment to foreground the 'personal voice' of Australian South Sea Islanders and a research process that would be 'driven by community' (ibid., p. 2). Through the engagement between community and researchers, this approach would honour the Pacific Islands culture of reciprocity.

Responsibility for the dilution of Australian South Sea Islander community agency in the articulation of our project for the final funding application cannot, however, be laid solely at the feet of the ARC. A review of the early draft material betrays an underlying positioning of ourselves as initiators of the project who, based on our scholarly expertise and personal links with the Australian South Sea Islander community, identified an opportunity for research and recognised its instrumental potential to deliver benefits that could help address a range of social and economic inequities experienced by people of Australian South Sea Islander heritage. In addition to providing high-impact scholarly outputs (arguably most beneficial to the chief investigators and partner investigators themselves), the project was designed to '*provide* Australian South Sea Islanders with tools, information and skills which will *empower them* to have stewardship over their own heritage and the ability to interpret and reinterpret their own histories in the long term' (Flexner, Miller & Mate, 2016, p. 3, emphasis added). The capacity-building goal inherent in the research was, therefore, rationalised as a potent political intervention, perhaps satisfying researcher-led moral commitments to correcting historical injustices as much as it was directed to fulfilling a community-led desire for the project.

Next steps (treading carefully)

In 2003, UNESCO officially recognised the value of cultural 'practices, representations, expressions, knowledge, [and] skills' (UNESCO, 2003, p. 2) in the Convention for the Safeguarding of the Intangible Cultural Heritage, which underscored cultural performance as an essential ingredient in sustaining cultural diversity, identity and creativity in the face of globalisation. In the context of research, this implies that communities need to be involved in the identification, interpretation, documentation and communication of their cultural practices as a form of living heritage. While scholarly researchers can help facilitate these processes through their methodological and project management know-how, community heritage research that is driven by external 'experts' makes little sense if the genuine objective is to support the vitality and perpetuation of lived cultures.

Taking its cue from the efforts of Australian South Sea Islanders to gain official recognition for their community as a distinct and significant cultural group in Queensland, our project emerged through early consultations with Australian South Sea Islander groups and an ethical commitment to sustaining their authority and ownership of the research. Differences between this community-led intent and how we were required to articulate the project for the purposes of ARC funding exposed a disconnect. In the context of CLR, there is a misalignment between the ways in which researchers envisage their professional identities in relation to other stakeholders and how those relationships are described and formalised in the official academic research system. Our project is further complicated through its focus on an Indigenous community that sits outside the remit of special provisions made for Aboriginal and Torres Strait Islander peoples in Australian heritage-related research.

Taken together, these tensions and discontinuities locate our particular project in a kind of research no-man's land, as we work with our Australian South Sea Islander partners to forge a fresh collaborative model that (at least ideally) can simultaneously satisfy the needs of academic scholarship and the community's agenda. How we define the concepts of researcher and research will continue to have profound implications for who benefits from the resources directed towards our project, as well as the new understandings of Australian South Sea Islander heritage that are produced through it. Our partnership with this community remains a work in progress, and the extent to which the wording of our approved ARC funding application will shape our unfolding collaboration is yet to be seen.

Acknowledgements

We would like to thank Australian South Sea Islander communities and community organisations in Mackay (especially MADASSIA), Ayr, Rockhampton and Joskeleigh for their ongoing participation and patience as this project develops. Research was funded through the University of Sydney Industry Engagement Fund (with contributions from Queensland Museum), and a grant from the Australian Research Council (LP170100048).

References

Anon., Personal communication (2017). Feedback: ARC LP application Flexner et al. (unpublished correspondence).
Australian Research Council (ARC). (2016a). *Funding rules for schemes under the Linkage Programme (2016 edition).* Canberra: Australian Government.
Australian Research Council (ARC). (2016b). *Linkage projects: Instructions to applicants for funding commencing in 2017 (version 1).* Canberra: Australian Government.
Brown, S. (2008). Mute or mutable? Archaeological significance, research and cultural heritage management in Australia. *Australian Archaeology, 67*(1), pp. 19–30.
Byrne, D. R. (2003). Nervous landscapes: Race and space in Australia. *Journal of Social Archaeology, 3*(2), pp. 169–193.
Queensland Government (2000). *Queensland Government action plan: Australian South Sea Islander community – from commitment to action* (brochure). Brisbane: Queensland Department of the Premier and Cabinet.
Beattie, P., Hollis, R. & Borbidge, R. (2000). *Queensland Government recognition statement: Australian South Sea Islander community.* 7 September. Brisbane: Queensland Government.

Flexner, J., Miller, I. & Mate, G. (2016). ASSI ARC Application Draft 28.10.2016 (unpublished).

Flexner, J. L., Mate, G., Miller, I., Prangnell, J., Robinson, H., Baumgartl, T. & Fairbairn, A. (2017). Australian Research Council Linkage Projects proposal for funding commencing in 2017: Archaeology, collections and Australian South Sea Islander lived identities (unpublished).

Gonzalez, S. L., Kretzler, I. & Edwards, B. (2018). Imagining indigenous and archaeological futures: Building capacity with the Federated Tribes of Grande Ronde. *Archaeologies, 14*(1), pp. 85–114.

Greer, S. (2010). Heritage and empowerment: Community-based Indigenous cultural heritage in northern Australia. *International Journal of Heritage Studies, 16*(1–2), pp. 45–58.

Harrison, R. (2004). *Shared landscapes: Archaeologies of attachment and the pastoral industry in New South Wales.* Sydney: University of New South Wales Press.

Kukutai, T. & Taylor, J. (eds.) (2016). *Indigenous data sovereignty: Toward an agenda.* Acton: ANU Press.

Mackay & District Australian South Sea Islander Association (MADASSIA) & Waite, S. (2000). *Protocols guide.* Mackay: Mackay & District Australian South Sea Islander Association.

Mackay & District Australian South Sea Islander Association (MADASSIA) (2019). Mackay & District Australian South Sea Islander Association Inc. (MADASSIA): About us, at My Community Directory (website). http://bit.ly/2OBiKsQ.

Meskell, L. A. (2013). UNESCO and the fate of the World Heritage Indigenous Peoples Council of Experts (WHIPCOE). *International Journal of Cultural Property, 20*(2), pp. 155–174.

National Health and Medical Research Council (NHMRC) (2018). *Ethical conduct in research with Aboriginal and Torres Strait Islander Peoples and communities: Guidelines for researchers and stakeholders.* Canberra: Commonwealth of Australia. https://bit.ly/2PxHyCf.

New South Wales Government (2010). *Cultural Connections: Indigenous communities managing biological and cultural diversity for ecological, cultural and economic benefit.* Sydney: NSW Department of Environment, Climate Change and Water.

Prangnell, J. (2013). Daughter of the sun. *International Journal of Historical Archaeology, 17*(3), pp. 423–427.

Robinson, H. (2017a). Project journal memo, 13 April (unpublished).

Robinson, H. (2017b). Project journal memo, 5 May (unpublished).

Robinson, H. (2017c). Project meeting minutes, 8 August (unpublished).

Smith, C. & Jackson, G. (2006). Decolonizing indigenous archaeology: Developments from down under. *American Indian Quarterly, 30*(3–4), pp. 311–349.

United Nations (2007). *United Nations Declaration on the Rights of Indigenous Peoples: Resolution adopted by the General Assembly on 13 September 2007.* New York: United Nations Secretariat. https://bit.ly/3cbgCzV.

United Nations Educational, Scientific and Cultural Organization (UNESCO) (2003). *Convention for the Safeguarding of the Intangible Cultural Heritage.* Paris: UNESCO.

Walter, M. (2016). Data politics and Indigenous representation in Australian statistics. In Kukutai, T. & J. Taylor (Eds.), *Indigenous data sovereignty: Toward an agenda,* pp. 79–98. Acton: ANU Press.

Veth, P., Mcdonald, J., Ward, I., O'Leary, M., Beckett, E., Benjamin, J., Ulm, S., Hacker, J., Ross, P. J. & Bailey, G. (2019). A strategy for assessing continuity in terrestrial and maritime landscapes from Murujuga (Dampier Archipelago), North West Shelf, Australia. *The Journal of Island and Coastal Archaeology, 15*(4), pp. 477–503. doi: 10.1080/15564894.2019.1572677.

6
Who steers the canoe? Community-led field archaeology in Vanuatu

James L. Flexner

The notion of 'community archaeology' has been around since at least the 1990s, though the idea that archaeology can and should involve people from living communities has been around for much longer than that (Marshall, 2002). Definitions and actual practices vary to some degree. 'Community' is often implicitly framed as something well defined and cohesive, while in practice community can be amorphous, fractious, and will mean different things to different people. Relationships with community vary as well, from consultations, sometimes seen as cynical 'tick-box' exercises (La Salle & Hutchings, 2018), to serious, long-term collaborations aimed at building real capacity for marginalised people (e.g. Gonzalez, Kretzler & Edwards, 2018).

In the Australasian region, community archaeology has been a robust part of the discipline (Marshall, 2002, p. 214), with leading scholars coming from Australia (e.g. Greer, 2010) and New Zealand (e.g. Allen et al., 2002) particularly. Here too the idea of community -based research is not without its critics, especially when regarding developer-led commercial archaeology (Zorzin, 2014). Nonetheless, there has been significant goodwill among archaeologists to work

J.L. Flexner (2021). Who steers the canoe? Community-led field archaeology in Vanuatu. In V. Rawlings, J. Flexner & L. Riley (Eds.), *Community-Led Research: Walking new pathways together*. Sydney: Sydney University Press.

closely with communities, particularly Indigenous communities, since at least the 1990s. In the Pacific Islands, where many archaeologists based in Australasian institutions do their work, community-oriented projects can be quite important (e.g. Crosby, 2002), though much of this potential has yet to be realised (Kawelu & Pakele, 2014).

In this chapter, I reflect on my work in Vanuatu since 2011, what it might offer in terms of our understanding of how a community-led archaeology can work, and what its limitations are. I want to challenge the notion of a 'decolonising' potential for community-led archaeology in light of the very real differences in power and wealth between local people, archaeologists, and the bodies that fund international research projects. Decolonising research is a concept that largely derives from Tuhiwai Smith's (2012) critique of research and re-articulation of an Indigenous research agenda. The idea of decolonising archaeology has been proposed in the Aboriginal Australian context (e.g. Smith & Jackson, 2006), and globally there has been a more general turn towards postcolonial archaeologies (e.g. Lydon & Rizvi, 2010). However, the optimism of a decade ago is increasingly challenged as in practice the promises of postcolonial or decolonising archaeology fail to live up to the theoretical possibilities (see Schmidt & Pikirayi, 2018). What I argue here is that archaeology can't necessarily escape its colonial past, but the knowledge we produce has a mostly unrealised decolonising potential only once that knowledge has been removed from the control of archaeologists and placed in the hands of communities.

Community-oriented or community-led?

I am going to distinguish between two types of community archaeology: community-oriented and community-led. I argue that most self-identified community archaeology is community-oriented. The archaeologist goes and lives or works within a community, however defined, and because everyone gets along and feels good about the project, it is considered a community archaeology project. This statement is not meant as a critique; it is a perfectly fine way to do archaeology. But in most cases, for a variety of reasons, the archaeologists ultimately set the agenda, albeit often with a sensitivity for community concerns and interests.

These types of relationships are particularly complicated in developer-led contract archaeology (Gnecco & Dias, 2015). Contract archaeology is the largest employer of professional archaeologists globally, originally emerging as a response to heritage legislation in wealthy countries in North America and Europe, but increasingly a global occupation (Shepherd, 2015). In many cases there is sincere will from the archaeologists to do some good by a community, particularly when working with Indigenous peoples, but the nature of developer -driven practice often places the archaeologist in a position of conflict of interest. The developer pays their salary and has certain requirements, which may or may not fit community desires or values. There can also be a tension where local communities in fact want development to go ahead, and the archaeology is perceived as a hindrance holding back a new road, building project, or industrial operation that people believe will create jobs. There is of course a larger critical discussion to be had about archaeology and its place within a capitalist order, but this is slightly beyond the scope of this chapter (Hutchings & La Salle, 2015; Zorzin, 2015).

In standard community-oriented projects, archaeologists give community some control over the archaeological process but ultimately it is the archaeological expert(s) who make the final decisions and control the design, the doing of the project, and the outputs. Community-led projects, in contrast, offer communities the ultimate decision-making power at all stages of the process. This includes the option to go back and revisit elements of the research design, and even the option to walk away from the project altogether if the community are not satisfied with how things are proceeding or if they feel the researcher is not delivering what was agreed upon. At the moment, truly community-led archaeology projects are extremely rare (Gonzalez et al., 2018 provide one example). The reasons for this include the development orientation of contract archaeology, and the 'fast-science', output-oriented approach to academic archaeology, which rewards results rather than the building of real relationships within a research setting (for a proposed alternative, see Cunningham & MacEachern, 2016).

In my own research in Vanuatu, I recognise elements of Community-Led Research (CLR); however, there is still much work to be done, and I am experimenting with how far a Community-led approach can be pushed within institutional limitations in current projects (see Robinson, Flexner & Miller, this volume). Cultural research was politicised in post-independence Vanuatu in a way that requires community leadership (discussed below). However, there are still very real differences in terms of wealth, access to resources, and access to information between Vanuatu and the neighbouring countries that fund research, including Australia. These differences can in some cases create a power differential between researchers and local people. That said, in my experience Vanuatu does tend to strike a reasonably good balance when giving communities the upper hand in cultural research.

Archaeological research in Vanuatu

Vanuatu (Figure 6.1) is a small island nation in the western Pacific, located about 2000 km east from Cape York Peninsula in north-eastern Australia. It sits at the crossroads between the Solomon Islands, New Caledonia and Fiji, and has for 3000 years been a major hub of human settlement and interaction (Bedford 2006; Bedford & Spriggs, 2014). The archipelago's current population of about 280,000 features some of the highest linguistic diversity in the world, with estimates ranging at 80 to 100 languages (Crowley, 2000; François, 2012), probably more before Europeans arrived beginning in the 1770s.

In terms of its colonial history, Vanuatu (called the New Hebrides from 1774–1980) saw its first major incursions of missionaries and other colonisers beginning in the 1840s (Flexner, 2016; Shineberg, 1966). Formal colonial status was not established until the 1880s, when an Anglo-French naval protectorate was established, formally transformed into a 'Condominium' government in 1906 (Jacomb, 1914). Colonialism wrought major changes in Vanuatu, from significant demographic upheaval due to introduced disease (McArthur, 1981) to dispossession and transformation of relationships to land (Van Trease, 1987). Vanuatu achieved independence in 1980, though not before significant conflict and struggle (Jolly, 1992).

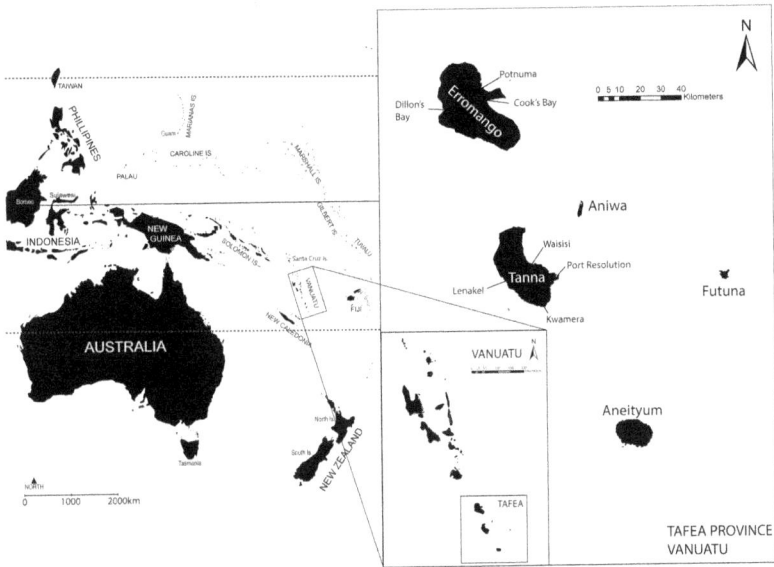

Figure 6.1 Map of Vanuatu and its context in the western Pacific, including detail of southern islands and locations mentioned in the text. (Flexner, adapted from Vanuatu Department of Lands basemaps)

Vanuatu's colonial and independence histories are relevant because these experiences shaped the post-independence attitude to research. The New Hebrides had a history as an anthropologists' playground (Adams, 1987), where many researchers from overseas would come, spend time 'studying' local communities, and then disappear over the horizon, never to be heard from again, though of course many other anthropologists also developed deep and real personal relationships with their hosts. Nonetheless, an independent Vanuatu sought better outcomes and better relationships. Beginning shortly after independence in 1980, there was a 'moratorium' on cultural research, which was lifted in 1994 with the Vanuatu Kaljoral Senta (Vanuatu Cultural Centre, hereafter VKS) placed as the primary mediator between communities and outside researchers (Taylor & Thieberger, 2011).

Cultural research as well as documentary filmmaking in Vanuatu now require a special permit from VKS. Significantly, the permit's conditions rely on the notion that a host community has a specific interest in the proposed research project, and that the project's outcomes will benefit the community in some way. How this is defined is dependent on conversations between researcher and community, usually mediated through the national network of *filwokas* (fieldworkers), usually community-appointed liaisons associated with VKS. *Filwokas* are indispensable cultural knowledge-holders, speakers of local languages, and usually the first point of contact between communities and researcher, or vice versa.

There is a long history of community-oriented archaeological research in Vanuatu, arguably stretching back to José Garanger's pathbreaking work in the 1960s (Garanger, 1996). The establishment of the Vanuatu Cultural and Historical Sites Survey in 1990, a few years before the lifting of the research moratorium, importantly aimed not only to document and conserve historical sites, but also to train Indigenous Ni-Vanuatu as cultural researchers to manage their own heritage. Subsequent workshops and training exercises have further developed the archaeological capabilities of various Ni-Vanuatu individuals and communities, particularly among the *filwokas* (see Bedford, Spriggs, Regenvanu & Yona, 2011; Willie 2019). Today archaeology in Vanuatu is to some degree community-led, although as will be explored below, the realities of differential access to resources and information maintain some degree of inequality that should prevent us feeling too comfortable about the situation.

From lecture hall to nakamal

It was in this collaborative archaeological research environment that I first encountered Vanuatu in 2011. My PhD from Berkeley (Flexner, 2010) focused on Hawai'ian archaeology, and I had a general idea that community was important, although it was something I'd only vaguely developed in my graduate research. As a fresh-faced young researcher, I was invited by Australian academics, speaking for *filwokas* and *jifs* (chiefs) in the southern islands of Tanna and Erromango, to begin a project exploring the archaeology of mission sites dating from the 1850s onwards (Flexner, 2016). With funding from the university in the US where I was teaching at the time, I booked a plane ticket and, knowing little about what to expect, off I flew to Vanuatu. That first season was a classic misadventure, involving lost luggage, cultural misunderstanding, and linguistic confusion (Flexner, 2018), but it was an important experience in shaping my perspectives on what community-led can mean in a decolonising Pacific.

I arrived initially in the capital, Port Vila, in June 2011. After spending a few days getting oriented and organising things like local currency and a few last-minute supplies I'd forgotten to pack, I boarded the small plane to Erromango. As the crew offloaded the luggage, I was alarmed to find that my bags, including the one I had accidentally packed my mobile phone in, had not come with me. Worse, the *filwoka* who I was told would meet me was nowhere to be found. Thus it was with some nervousness that I watched the plane depart the small grass strip, not scheduled to return for another five days. Having been in the country only a few days, my Bislama (the local pidgin language) was non-existent. Luckily there was a self-identified 'chief' from Ipota, at the time the only airport on the island, who spoke enough English to figure out who I was and what I wanted. White visitors to Erromango were, and are, fairly rare, and Americans even rarer. It took a bit of explaining that I was not, in fact, a Peace Corps volunteer, and that I was there on a research permit from VKS.

Eventually, Jerry Taki, the senior *filwoka* for Erromango, did arrive. We used his mobile to contact colleagues in Port Vila to try to track down my bags, which did, eventually, appear a week later. That settled, as the sun began to set in Ipota, Jerry told me he wanted to do a 'ceremony' to welcome me to the island. As we sat on the grass just behind the airport terminal building, he got out what appeared to be a stick of some sort and started chewing. Eventually a masticated wad of fibre was spat onto a leaf. This was strained with fresh water through a cloth, which looked clean enough, into a coconut shell, and was offered to me to … drink. At this stage I basically realised I was either going to drink the shell or I wouldn't make it in Vanuatu. So, I obliged and politely smiled after downing the greyish, metallic tasting liquid.

What Jerry had offered me was my first shell of truly traditional kava, an intoxicating beverage made from the *Piper methysticum* plant, which is essential to male sociality throughout Vanuatu (Brunton, 1989; Siméoni & Lebot, 2014). It is, in hindsight, quite likely that Jerry had been late to meet me at the airport because he had dug up this root from his own garden, which was several hours' walk from Ipota. This fairly simple gesture is a classic example of establishing a relationship of reciprocity (Mauss, 1990), one which would last for many years during and beyond this particular project. It also established Jerry as the instigator of the relationship, representing the community on Erromango. In other words, the welcome involving a shell of kava, something I have subsequently experienced in nearly every village I've visited in the five islands of south Vanuatu, puts the outside researcher in a position of obligation to the local people from the outset.

The following day, I paid for a charter boat, the typical seven-metre fibreglass model with outboard motor used throughout Vanuatu, to take us around to the west coast of the island and the village of Williams' Bay (formerly Dillon's Bay, renamed after the London Missionary Society missionary who was killed at that place in 1839). On the way, we trawled with a lure behind the boat and caught a large wahoo. Once again, this was a significant catch, as upon our arrival the fish was divided up, with the chiefs (*Fan lo*) in Dillon's Bay taking the best portions. We also kept a portion for ourselves which we cooked with 'local curry' (bush spices) and ate for lunch that day. These simple principles of reciprocity and conviviality, sharing of resources and of meals, are critical elements of community-led work in Vanuatu, as I'm sure they are in many parts of the world. They are the building blocks for developing trust and common ground, which are a foundation to doing CLR.

I had been invited to Dillon's Bay to document the historical archaeology of John Williams, and the subsequent Presbyterian missionaries George Gordon and H. A. Robertson. As it turned out, my baggage being taken to the wrong island had been a blessing. I arrived with a basic GPS for recording site locations, a notebook and little else as my equipment was in my other bags. What this meant was that rather than launching straight into the technical aspects of my work, I spent my first five days in Dillon's Bay simply walking around

Figure 6.2 Clearing a memorial enclosure near Dillon's Bay during archaeological survey. From left to right, Jerry Taki, Manuel Naling, Malon Lovo and Thomas Poki.

with Jerry and local chiefs and elders from the Presbyterian church (Figure 6.2). This was instrumental to my understanding of how local people perceived the landscape in Dillon's Bay, and I used the same approach to documenting other sites in this project (Flexner, 2014). I did my best to put community perspectives as I understood them first, then considered what kinds of archaeological techniques would be appropriate to reflect and complement those perspectives. The result was ultimately probably richer and more interesting than if I had simply followed the orthodox, technical approach to archaeological survey.

Community-led or spectator sport?

A few years after my initial fieldwork trip in Vanuatu, I experienced another illustrative episode of the way CLR works in the country. By 2013, I had shifted to Australia through a postdoctoral fellowship awarded by the Australian Research Council to expand on my mission archaeology work. That year, I was in Kwamera, a remote village in the far south of Tanna Island, excavating an 1880s mission house that had been inhabited by William and Agnes Watt (Flexner, 2016, pp. 98–107). Unexpectedly, we began uncovering fragments of human bone from beneath the front step of the mission house.

In Hawai'i, *iwi kūpuna* (ancestral remains) are highly sacred, and how they are handled by archaeologists is a major concern for *kanaka māoli* (Native Hawai'ians), who would generally prefer that human remains simply be left to rest (Kawelu, 2007, pp. 99–111). With my previous experience in Hawai'i, I therefore expected this would be the point where I was told by the community that I was no longer welcome. I was quite surprised then when the local people I was working with suggested the opposite. They wanted to see the bones, understand who was buried there, and how long ago. I explained that at that point, I in fact didn't have the right equipment to excavate a burial, but could stop excavations, backfill the trench, and return the following year to investigate further.

The community assented, and in 2014 I returned, this time with Indigenous VKS archaeologist Edson Willie, who had just completed a degree in archaeology from the University of Papua New Guinea. Edson and I, prepared this time for what we would encounter, began carefully uncovering the skeleton. The only caveat the community had was that if we had to leave excavations open overnight, we should cover the bones with some dirt to prevent the *ierehma* (spirit) of the deceased from walking around and potentially causing harm. We did this, and over a few days we uncovered a single individual who was buried in an extended, supine position but whose bones had fairly badly deteriorated in the black beach sands. The burial turned out to be roughly 800 years old, and offers material to reflect on an interesting story about where missionaries were placed by local people when setting up the house and church (Flexner & Willie, 2015).

At one point during our excavation, one of the student volunteers took a photograph of our work in action that is a fairly typical scene in Vanuatu archaeology (Figure 6.3), though we perhaps had a bigger crowd than usual for the skeleton excavation on the church ground just outside the main village. But normally archaeology in Vanuatu is very much a public event. We hire local people to excavate with us, and often curious passers-by will stop for a few minutes or even a few hours to watch what we're doing, ask questions, tell stories, and make small-talk. The *filwokas* are usually well known and respected members of the community where the work is taking place, so will have close personal connections to the people around us. Everyone from adults walking to and from gardens, to children on their way to or from school, will stop for a chat. In some cases, we even put them to work. Particularly for students, I make a point of making sure that if they're hanging around the trench, they're also learning something (whether they actually pay attention to me is another story).

People are curious about this exotic way of digging a hole very slowly with small hand tools punctuated by many stops to record notes, take photographs, and draw. It is also an opportunity for villagers to meet people from overseas, and many who have been abroad (usually to work as farm labourers) will proudly tell you about their adventures in Australia and New Zealand. The point here is that what people take away from CLR is not necessarily what the research itself is about. In some cases, the people who stop to talk to us are not really that interested in archaeology or the past at all. Rather, it's an opportunity to see something novel and talk to some people who they don't normally interact with. As researchers, we should be fine with this. Not everyone is necessarily interested in the particular niche fields we find so fascinating, and we can't force them to be. But building those kinds of personal, friendly relationships is another foundational element of CLR in Vanuatu, and in some cases, what begins as a simple friendship might develop into a more profound interest in the topic(s) at hand.

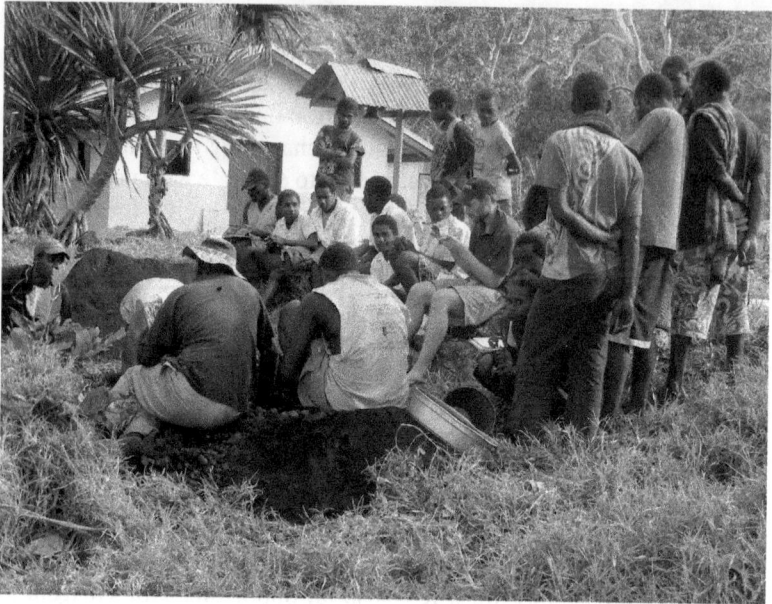

Figure 6.3 A big crowd gathers to watch Edson Willie and me excavating, Kwamera, Tanna.

Making the most of a ruined church

As a final vignette in community-led archaeology in Vanuatu, I turn to a church building from Lenakel, on the west coast of Tanna. The church was a prefabricated kit, imported from Australia by the Presbyterian Mission and erected in 1912 (Flexner et al., 2015). This was a key site in my initial work on Tanna. The community of Lenakel were rightly concerned about the building, which had deteriorated through a combination of damage from termites and tropical rainstorms to the point that it had to be officially closed after New Year's Eve, 2000.

Over two years, under the tutelage of Martin Jones, an expert standing buildings archaeologist from New Zealand, we documented the Lenakel church intensively, to the point that it's probably the most well-recorded colonial building of its type in Melanesia. We prepared a

Statement of Significance for the Presbyterian Church, and were in the process of figuring out how to find resources for a restoration project when Tropical Cyclone Pam ripped through Vanuatu in March 2015, featuring sustained winds of over 280 km/h. The Lenakel church was completely destroyed in this event.

I was in Vanuatu a few months later, in July 2015, and made a trip to Lenakel partly to check in with friends on Tanna to see how they were doing after the cyclone, and partly to see how the site looked after the storm. I had some trepidation about facing the local community. Would they blame me for the lack of action to restore the church before the cyclone? How could I explain that my research grant didn't include funding for this type of activity, and that finding a funding source that would support such work was a time-consuming process? I did feel a bit guilty about not doing more on this front, but academic demands mean one can only spend time on so many projects. To my great relief, there was no such feeling among the community and I was welcomed warmly and with open arms to west Tanna as usual.

If anything, people remained optimistic that something could be done with the site. In part, this is a reflection of the intangible heritage of the place, which I've argued is more important than the 'authentic' built fabric of the old church, now largely destroyed and dispersed (Flexner et al., 2016). From a community-led perspective, I also wonder if part of the work we did added to the prestige of the site. After all, people came from all over the world to work on this particular building in Lenakel, and so it is doing its work as an important *kastom* place, bringing together the traditional and the modern. One of the local chiefly titles is *Nikiatu*, which is the name for the beam that connects the outrigger to the main canoe hull. It is, among other things, a metaphor for those who bring Tanna together with the outside world. Perhaps the church served a similar purpose in local people's minds. That it was still getting attention as a ruin reflected the fact that the place and its stories remained important, even if the building itself was gone.

Another element of CLR is not to put too much pressure on ourselves as researchers to do *everything* the community might ask of us. Having largely left behind my work on the Tanna church, it is no longer up to me to decide what happens to the site going forward. In fact, it never was. Rather, the people of Lenakel can and should decide how to 'manage' their heritage, particularly as Tanna changes rapidly in the face of ongoing development (Flexner et al., 2018).

Can archaeology decolonise?

In southern Vanuatu, the land divisions on most islands are referred to as 'canoes' (Erromango *lo*; Tanna *neteta, niko*; Aneityum *nelcau*). One chiefly role in these spaces is to 'steer', to direct the people living in the territory in a way that maintains consensus and harmony. As an outsider entering such spaces, my role is to temper my interests against an understanding of what direction the community want to take, how the canoe should be steered in other words, largely negotiated through the *filwokas*, chiefs and elders. It is by no means a perfect system, but it offers some sense of shared power in shaping a research process.

Vanuatu, through the leadership of the VKS, provides one example of how to beneficially balance community-led interests against those of foreign researchers. Generally, communities are given the upper hand, and empowered through the *filwokas* to find people to work on projects that they perceive as beneficial in some way. However, I don't want to paint too rosy a portrait of these relationships. While I've offered some generally positive vignettes to illustrate how things work overall, there have certainly been plenty of tense moments and complicated negotiations in my nine years working in Vanuatu's southern islands.

One of the ongoing problems in attempting to do community-led work in Vanuatu is the fact that there are still very real differences in the level of wealth between 'there' and 'here'. The Australian Research Council has, over the years, funded Vanuatu archaeology to the tune of millions of dollars, and significant amounts of this money go to paying for local room and board and hiring local workers, including the *filwokas*, all of whom work for a tiny fraction of what is considered minimum wage in Australia. This problem of hiring local labour has been a topic of discussion in archaeology for some time (e.g. Matsuda, 1998) and I don't want to dwell on it too much other than for what it means for CLR. Hiring local people is appropriate for a number of reasons, but is a site of negotiation. It is also a source of tension in communities, and in my experience the best cases are those where local chiefs and families decide who is to work on the project, often selecting people to rotate so there's a sense that the work has been shared fairly throughout the village.

This still leaves a power differential with which I am not entirely comfortable. If I'm paying people as labourers, how much will they really tell me what they do and don't want me to do? Nonetheless, I also wouldn't want to simply bring in groups of students to dig without having local people alongside them in the trenches, and if locals are working, they should be paid for their time. It's an intractable problem, and as noted above, probably one of those irresolvable contradictions inherent to capitalism. I think it is telling in terms of CLR that there is nonetheless an element of reciprocal exchange to these interactions. Yes, I often find myself handing out what for local people are relatively large sums of cash at the end of a project. But on the other side are usually local goods such as woven pandanus baskets or shell necklaces, and of course a feast involving many shells of kava to close things on a happy note (Flexner, 2019).

This is still where I think we hit the limits of what is possible in terms of decolonising archaeology. Ironically, the apparent wealth differentials are to some degree a result of extractive industry during the colonial era. One period account records the equivalent of approximately £19,000,000 worth of sandalwood in contemporary currency removed from Erromango between the 1850s and the early 1900s (Robertson, 1902, p. 34). The Erromangans were paid in cheap trade goods, if at all, with most of that wealth concentrating in Australia and Britain. There is simply too much of the old colonial order in the contemporary distribution of wealth.

Then there is the production and distribution of knowledge. I sit typing on my laptop in a Sydney suburb, with near-instantaneous access through a major university library to most of the world's academic research. While people in Vanuatu increasingly have access to the internet through mobile phones and tablets, the ability to access reliable information, and to understand the notion of research, remains highly limited. Formal education is, somewhat ironically, very expensive for many people as public education in Vanuatu requires parents to pay annual school fees. Few people complete a secondary education, an even smaller number attend university, and currently there are three

Indigenous Ni-Vanuatu with any formal tertiary education for archaeology specifically.

We carry too much colonial baggage to be able to claim archaeology is a truly decolonising discipline. The discipline itself still can't completely escape its aim of documenting and ordering past human activities and accomplishments according to systematic, rigorous standards, and this ordering is itself, arguably, a reflection of a somewhat colonial mindset. If we really want to have a decolonising archaeology, we have to let go of the information we produce and place it in the hands of the communities we work with, and even then there's a long way to go. We can start with things like open-access publications, and offering programs in local schools (although this is complicated; Bezzerra, 2015). Ultimately, we are also going to have to start pushing against, and probably dismantling, the world order that shapes what is possible in a variety of small and probably much bigger ways, a conversation that will have to happen in far more radical ways than the small seeds of a community-led archaeology examined here.

Acknowledgements

I have so many people to thank for this research. For this particular paper I'd like to thank specifically Matthew Spriggs, who got me to Vanuatu in the first place, the late Jerry Taki, who introduced me to Erromango and was a valuable colleague and mentor, the late Jacob Kapere, an instrumental *filwoka* from Tanna and scholar in his own right, Samson Ieru and Robert Steven in Kwamera, and Chief Peter Marshall and Iavis Nikiatu from Lenakel.

References

Adams, R. (1987). Homo anthropologicus and Man-Tanna: Jean Guiart and the anthropological attempt to understand the Tannese. *Journal of Pacific History,* *22*(1), pp. 3–14.

Allen, H., Johns, D., Phillips, C., Day, K., O'Brien, T., & Mutunga, N. (2002). Wahi Ngaro (the lost portion): Strengthening relationships between people and wetlands in North Taranaki, New Zealand. *World Archaeology, 34*(2), pp. 315–329.

Bedford, S. (2006). *Pieces of the Vanuatu puzzle: Archaeology of the north, south, and centre.* Canberra: ANU Press.

Bedford, S., Spriggs, M., Regenvanu, R. & Yona, S. (2011). Olfala histri we i stap andanit long graon. Archaeological training workshops in Vanuatu: A profile, the benefits, spin-offs, and extraordinary discoveries. In J. Taylor & N. Thieberger (Eds.), *Working together in Vanuatu: Research histories, collaborations, projects and reflections,* pp. 191–213. Canberra: ANU Press.

Bedford, S. & Spriggs, M. (2014). The archaeology of Vanuatu: 3000 years of history across islands of ash and coral. In E. Cochrane & T. Hunt (Eds.), *Oxford handbook of prehistoric Oceania,* pp. 1–17. Oxford: Oxford University Press.

Bezerra, M. (2015). At that edge: Archaeology, heritage education, and human rights in the Brazilian Amazon. *International Journal of Historical Archaeology, 19*(4), pp. 822–831.

Brunton, Ron. (1989). *The abandoned narcotic: Kava and cultural instability in Melanesia.* Cambridge: Cambridge University Press.

Crosby, A. (2002). Archaeology and vanua development in Fiji. *World Archaeology, 34*(2), pp. 363–378.

Crowley, T. (2000). The language situation in Vanuatu. *Current Issues in Language Planning, 1*(1), pp. 47–132.

Cunningham, J. J. & MacEachern, S. (2016). Ethnoarchaeology as slow science. *World Archaeology, 48*(5), pp. 628–641. doi: 10.1080/00438243.2016.1260046.

Flexner, J. L. (2010). *Archaeology of the recent past at Kalawao: Landscape, place, and power in a Hawai'ian Leprosarium* (doctoral dissertation). Berkely: University of California, Berkeley.

Flexner, J. L. (2014). Mapping local perspectives in the historical archaeology of Vanuatu mission landscapes. *Asian Perspectives, 53*(1), pp. 2–28.

Flexner, J. L. (2016). *An archaeology of early christianity in Vanuatu: Kastom and religious change on Tanna and Erromango, 1839–1920.* Canberra: ANU Press.

Flexner, J. L. (2018). Doing archaeology in non-state space. *Journal of Contemporary Archaeology, 5*(2), pp. 254–259.

Flexner, J. L. (2019). 'With the consent of the tribe': Marking lands on Tanna and Erromango, New Hebrides. *History and Anthropology.* doi: 10.1080/02757206.2019.1607732.

Flexner, J. L., Jones, M. J. & Evans, P. D. (2015). 'Because it is a holy house of God': Buildings archaeology, globalization, and community heritage in a Tanna church. *International Journal of Historical Archaeology, 19*(2), pp. 262–288.

Flexner, J. L., Jones, M. J. & Evans, P. D. (2016). Destruction of the 1912 Lenakel church (Tanna, Vanuatu) and thoughts for the future of the site. *International Journal of Historical Archaeology, 20*(2), pp. 463–469. doi: 10.1007/ s10761-015-0304-7.

Flexner, J. L., Lindstrom, L., Hickey, F. R. & Kapere, J. (2018). Kaio, kapwier, nepek, and nuk: Human and non-human agency, and 'conservation' on Tanna, Vanuatu. In B. Verschuuren & S. Brown (Eds.), *Cultural and spiritual significance of nature in protected areas: Governance, management and policy*, pp. 253–265. London: Routledge.

Flexner, J. L. & Willie, E. (2015). Under the mission steps: An 800 year-old human burial from south Tanna, Vanuatu. *Journal of Pacific Archaeology, 6*(2), pp. 49–55.

François, A. (2012). The dynamics of linguistic diversity: Egalitarian multilingualism and power imbalance among northern Vanuatu languages. *International Journal of the Sociology of Language, 214*, pp. 85–110.

Garanger, J. (1996). Tongoa, Mangaasi and Retoka: History of a prehistory. In J. Bonnemaison, K. Huffman, C. Kaufmann & D. Tryon (Eds.), *Arts of Vanuatu*, pp. 66–73. Honolulu: University of Hawai'i Press.

Gnecco, C. & Dias, A. S. (2015). On contract archaeology. *International Journal of Historical Archaeology, 19*(4), pp. 687–698.

Gonzalez, S. L., Kretzler, I. & Edwards, B. (2018). Imagining Indigenous and archaeological futures: Building capacity with the Federated Tribes of Grande Ronde. *Archaeologies, 14*(1), pp. 85–114.

Greer, S. (2010). Heritage and empowerment: Community-based Indigenous cultural heritage in northern Australia. *International Journal of Heritage Studies, 16*(1–2), pp. 45–58.

Hutchings, R. & La Salle, M. (2015). Archaeology as disaster capitalism. *International Journal of Historical Archaeology, 19*(4), pp. 699–720.

Jacomb, E. (1914). *France and England in the New Hebrides*. Melbourne: George Robertson.

Jolly, M. (1992). Custom and the way of the land: Past and present in Vanuatu and Fiji. *Oceania, 62*(4), pp. 330–354.

Kawelu, K. L. (2007). *A sociopolitical history of Hawai'ian archaeology: Kuleana and commitment* (doctoral dissertation). Berkeley: University of California, Berkeley.

Kawelu, K. L, & Pakele, D. (2014). Community-based research: The next step in Hawai'ian archaeology. *Journal of Pacific Archaeology, 5*(2), pp. 62–71.

La Salle, M. & Hutchings, R. (2018). 'What could be more reasonable?' Collaboration in colonial contexts. In A. M. Labrador & N. A. Silberman (Eds.), *The Oxford handbook of public erhitage theory and practice*, pp. 223–¬37. Oxford: Oxford University Press.

Lydon, J. & Rizvi, U. (Eds.) (2010). *Handbook of postcolonial archaeology*. Walnut Creek, CA: Left Coast Press.

Matsuda, D. (1998). The ethics of archaeology, subsistence digging, and artifact looting in Latin America: Point muted counterpoint. *International Journal of Cultural Property, 7*(1), pp. 87–97.

Marshall, Y. (2002). What is community archaeology? *World Archaeology, 34*(2), pp. 211–219.

Mauss, M. (1990). *The gift: The form and reason for exchange in archaic societies* (W. D. Halls, Trans.). London: Routledge.

McArthur, N. (1981). *New Hebrides population 1840–1967: A re-interpretation*. Noumea: South Pacific Commission.

Robertson, H. A. (1902). *Erromanga: The martyr isle*. Toronto: The Westminster Company.

Schmidt, P. R. & Pikirayi, I. (2018). Will historical archaeology escape its Western prejudices to become relevant to Africa? *Archaeologies, 14*(3), pp. 443–471. doi: 10.1007/s11759-018-9342-1.

Shepherd, N. (2015). Contract archaeology in South Africa: Traveling theory, local memory, and global designs. *International Journal of Historical Archaeology, 19*(4), pp. 748–763.

Shineberg, D. (1966). The sandalwood trade in Melanesian economics, 1841–1865. *Journal of Pacific History, 1*(1), pp. 129–146.

Siméoni, P & Lebot, V. (2014). *Buveurs de kava*. Port Vila: Éditions Géo-Consulte.

Smith, C. & Jackson, G. (2006). Decolonizing Indigenous archaeology: Developments from Down Under. In *American Indian Quarterly, 30*(3–4), pp. 311–349.

Taylor, J. & Thieberger, N. (Eds.) (2011). *Working together in Vanuatu: Research histories, collaborations, projects and reflections*. Canberra: ANU Press.

Tuhiwai Smith, L. (2012). *Decolonizing methodologies: Research and Indigenous peoples* (2nd ed.). New York: Zed Books.

Van Trease, H. (1987). *The politics of land in Vanuatu*. Suva: University of the South Pacific Press.

Willie, E. (2019). A Melanesian view of archaeology in Vanuatu. In M. Leclerc & J. Flexner (Eds.), *Archaeologies of Island Melanesia: Current approaches to landscapes, exchange, and practice*. pp. 211–214. Canberra: ANU Press.

Zorzin, N. (2014). Heritage management and Aboriginal Australians: Relations in a global, neoliberal economy – a contemporary case study from Victoria. *Archaeologies, 10*(2), pp. 132–167.

Zorzin, N. (2015). Archaeology and capitalism: Successful relationship or economic and ethical alienation? In C. Gnecco & D. Lippert (Eds.), *Ethics and archaeological praxis,* pp. 115–139. New York: Springer.

7

Researcher or student? Knowing when not to know in Community-Led Indigenous research

Sheelagh Daniels-Mayes

Methods of undertaking research and recruiting participants have traditionally been located within the cultural preferences and practices of the 'Western' world rather than the distinct cultural ways of the peoples being investigated (Bishop, 2011). Writing from a New Zealand perspective, Bishop goes on to argue (2011, p. 19):

> Maori people, along with many other minoritised peoples, are concerned that educational researchers have been slow to acknowledge the importance of culture and cultural differences as key components in successful research practice and understandings. As a result, key research issues of power relations, initiation, benefits, representation, legitimisation, and accountability continue to be addressed in terms of the researchers' own cultural agendas, concerns, and interests.

Likewise, Aboriginal peoples of Australia are concerned about how their distinct cultural ways of knowing, being and doing are to be

S. Daniels-Mayes (2021). Researcher or student? Knowing when not to know in Community-Led Indigenous research. In V. Rawlings, J. Flexner & L. Riley (Eds.), *Community-Led Research: Walking new pathways together.* Sydney: Sydney University Press.

not only recognised in research, but centrally positioned within the research process and outcomes (Rigney, 2006). Additionally, Aboriginal peoples are concerned about power relations, values, accountability, ownership, dissemination and benefits of the research (Fredericks, 2007; Gower, 2012).

By contrast to traditional methods of investigation, culturally responsive research focuses on respecting and privileging the ways of knowing, being and doing of participants in the research process (Berryman, SooHoo & Nevin, 2013). Thus, when research is approached from a culturally sensitive stance, the varied aspects of a distinct culture as well as the varied historical and contemporary experiences of a people are recognised. In this way, the shared knowledge and understandings of the phenomenon under study are privileged and the individual and collective/community knowledge is placed at the centre of the investigation (Daniels-Mayes, 2016). Likewise, Indigenous diplomatic protocols and practices are prioritised and observed (Daniels-Mayes & Sehlin MacNeil, 2019). In Karen Martin's (2008, p. 78) distinct Aboriginal cultural Ways of Being, she explains:

> Ultimately, Ways of Being hold for us processes for fulfilling relatedness with respect, responsibility and accountability. Where Ways of Knowing contextualise the Stories, Ways of Being ground these to ensure what we have learned and know is applied with respect, responsibility and accountability in a range of contexts and situations.

Furthermore, as a culturally responsive researcher, and more specifically as an Aboriginal culturally responsive researcher, there are protocols to be observed (ways of doing). For example, Moreton-Robinson (2000, p. xv) writes in her work:

> The protocol for introducing one's self to other Indigenous people is to provide information about one's cultural location, so that connection can be made on political, cultural and social grounds and relations established.

Positioning myself in my research is therefore the observation and enactment of cultural protocols. So let me introduce myself. For ease of conversation, I identify as being an Australian Aboriginal woman as many do not know my Country of Kamilaroi. I am a lecturer, researcher, educator, and scholarly advocate primarily in the spaces of Aboriginal education and disability. Over the years I have done much listening, reading, writing, thinking, questioning and learning, of self and others, that led me to the theoretical frameworks of cultural responsiveness (see, for example, Castagno & Brayboy, 2008; Gay, 2010; Ladson-Billings, 1994) and Critical Race Theory (see, for example, Ladson-Billings & Tate, 2006; Lynn, Yosso, Solórzano & Parker, 2002). This seeking of knowing has been the inadvertent enactment of what Kress (2011) refers to as Critical Praxis Research (CPR) that requires 'scholar–practitioners to develop critical consciousness about who they are in relation to their students and the larger society in order to then determine the best methods for conducting sophisticated research that is fair, ethical, and empowering for all stakeholders' (Kress, 2011, p. 10). With regards to my ethnographic research, the word 'student' in the above quote is replaced with 'community'. By privileging the 'community' within which I am working, their cultures, their knowledges, I am rejecting traditional colonising research methods and am instead being led by the needs and aspirations of the community. As with others throughout this volume, the aim is to make communities equal partners in the research process. A key question I use for focusing my CPR is: 'Would I want to be participating in my research? Why? Why not?' I also constantly critically reflect upon the given day's events to identify what is working and what lessons I learnt (a point I return to later in this chapter).

Research and context

This chapter uses Critical Praxis Research (Kress, 2011) to develop critical consciousness around a multi-sited school ethnography (Castagno, 2006) that had the following aim: to examine pedagogies in two mainstream secondary schools in metropolitan Adelaide that are both committed to improving academic outcomes for Aboriginal students and to reveal and develop a counterstory of Aboriginal education success. The research worked extensively with six community-nominated teachers (Foster, 1994; Ladson-Billings, 1994; McDonald, 2003) over two years of fieldwork. The participants taught across all year levels (and in South Australia that was from years 8 to 12), and subject disciplines, with teaching experience ranging from two years to over three decades. There were three male and three female teachers with one male identifying as being Aboriginal. Each school had an Aboriginal student population of at least 10 per cent (Australian Bureau of Statistics, 2010), which demonstrates Aboriginal community support but also means that they belonged to a minority culture within these schools.

This chapter is organised into two main sections following this introduction. First, I examine the purpose of research in Aboriginal spaces, focusing on problematising terra nullius–styled research, benefits of research, and ways of working ethically, socially and culturally. I will then turn to Part Two: Enacting culturally responsive research, with a focus on an accessible research vernacular; participant selection; and the consideration of insider or outsider. The chapter is intended to bring to

the fore key areas which my thinking and my practice, as an Indigenous/Aboriginal/Kamilaroi woman working in Aboriginal spaces, need to contend with. The chapter problematises the question: when do I know not to know and therefore become the student and not the researcher?

Part One: The purposes of research

Problematising terra nullius–styled research

Aboriginal scholars such as Martin (2003), Rigney (2006) and Gower (2012) contend that the extent of research in Australian Aboriginal lands and on Aboriginal peoples since colonisation in the late 18th century 'is so vast it makes Aboriginal peoples one of the most researched groups of people on earth' (Martin, 2003, p. 1). Investigations have been conducted by all manner of natural and social scientists, usually without permission, consultation or involvement of Aboriginal peoples (Bourke, 1999). Martin (2003, p. 1) writes of 'terra nullius' research:

In this research, we are present only as objects of curiosity and subjects of research. To be seen but not asked, heard nor respected. So the research has been undertaken in the same way Captain James Cook falsely claimed the eastern coast of the land to become known as Australia as terra nullius.

This fictional doctrine of terra nullius not only devalued, dispossessed and marginalised Aboriginal people but also set the scene for how relationships between Aboriginal and non-Aboriginal peoples within Australia were to operate (Matthews, 2012, p. 122). Moreover, Hart and Whatman (1998, p. 3) state that for over 200 years:

The premise of most [Western] research and analysis has been locked into the belief that Indigenous Australians are anachronisms and, in defiance of the laws of evolution, remain a curiosity of nature, and are 'fair game' for research. The overt and covert presumptions underwriting all [Western] research and analysis into Indigenous Australian cultures is the inherent view of the superiority of Non-Indigenous society's cultures.

Consequently, much research targeting Aboriginal peoples has sought to understand Aboriginal peoples and their cultures from the foundation of non-Aboriginal perspectives, methodologies and measures (Carlson, 2013). Such an approach is embedded in the majoritarian narrative of racism which excluded Aboriginal peoples from knowledge construction as defined by Western thought (Kovach, 2009). In this traditional approach to research, the investigator's way of knowing is privileged over the researched (Kress, 2011). Researchers, especially with their legacy of complicity with colonisation, need to engage in research that seeks to counter the colonising impact of research (Berryman, SooHoo & Nevin, 2013). This approach requires a shift in thinking and power that recognises that Aboriginal peoples should not be considered as being 'known', but rather recognised and respected as 'knowers' (Martin, 2008; Moreton-Robinson, 2011), with the investigator needing to enter the research project as a student ready and willing to learn from the knowers. Arguably, this is particularly important when undertaking research in Aboriginal contexts owing to the legacy of terra nullius–styled research where participants were considered to be subjects to be studied and no more.

Benefit of research

When undertaking research, I am ever-mindful of Indigenous researcher Shawn Wilson (Askwayak Cree from northern Manitoba, Canada), who asserts that 'Research is not just something that's out there: it's something that you're building for yourself and for your community' (2001, p. 179). I am also mindful of the words of Brayboy and Maughan (2009, p. 12) who state: 'Indigenous Knowledges requires responsible behaviour, and this is often achieved by considering the ramifications of actions before they are taken'. Finally, I am conscious of the words of educator and scholar Tyson Kaawoppa Yunkaporta, Bama man of Nunga and Koori descent, who argues that 'The protocol we follow in this work is, "If you take something, put something back"' (Yunkaporta & Kirby, 2011, p. 205). So, as an Indigenous/Aboriginal/ Kamilaroi researcher, I seek to put back more than I take when engaging in research. The primary aim of my work is for it to be of benefit to the participants and their communities, rather than being of disadvantage (AIATSIS, 2012). A culturally responsive approach seeks to counteract the devastating legacy of traditional Western research so that new knowledge and understandings can be acquired.

Ways of working culturally, ethically and socially

As my research progressed, several guiding principles emerged. First, my research needed to go beyond interpretivist ethnography that aims to simply advance knowledge with no further purpose or benefit. Second, my research demands that I am culturally, ethically and socially responsible to the participants and their communities. If I undertake my research without being relationally accountable to both the participants and to the wider community, I, like colonising researchers of the past, could do more harm. My research was not just about getting a PhD and moving on with my life, it was about doing it 'proper ways' (Aunty Nangala, personal communication, 23 June 2013). 'Proper ways' research is an Aboriginal English term that means that my research was mindful of working in ways that located the research within the cultural ways of knowing, being and doing of participants. It is an approach that privileges the valuable insider knowledge of research participants and their methodologies (Moreton-Robinson, 2011). Third, to be of benefit to participants, my investigation was formed and shaped by those consulted, a process repeated throughout the length of the project, as the communities involved led the research in a diversity of ways. Finally, my research needed to be of some tangible value to the Aboriginal community and not just using their stories for my own advancement as in terra nullius–styled research investigations.

Additionally, continual critical reflection on the research investigation played a pivotal role in the project's success. The following questions, adapted from Wilson (2008, p. 178), were frequently referred back to in my process of Critical Praxis Research:

- What is my purpose, intention and frame of analysis?
- How am I fulfilling my role in this relationship?
- What are my responsibilities in this relationship?
- How may I avoid doing harm?
- Does this method help to build a relationship between myself as a researcher and my participants?
- What will be left behind after I have completed my research?

Having established the need for Community-Led Research, I now discuss how the research was enacted, focusing on the examples of language, participant selection, and the tensions of insider and outsider status.

Part Two: Enacting culturally responsive research

An accessible research vernacular

Language is used to discuss, debate, exchange information and to communicate ideas. However, language is also a means for the enactment of exclusion, discrimination and prejudice, as cultural values and attitudes are reflected in the structures and meanings of the language we use (Flinders University, n.d.). Language, therefore, is not neutral or unproblematic. Wilson (2008, p. 279) writes that 'Language mastery can be used in a bad way to make people feel small, or it can be used in a good way to explain concepts'. Similarly, Basil Johnston, an Ojibwa storyteller, writes that 'Words are medicine that can heal or injure' (cited in Archibald, 2008, p. 19). Language is used to convey the research purpose, it is the means by which participants share their stories, and language is used to interpret and represent the narratives shared. But what language do I use to make the research accessible, and therefore valuable, to the participants and the wider community?

As a culturally responsive researcher, my responsibility is to draw on the language strengths of participants so as not to exclude or discriminate, nor ultimately to alienate. Moreover, drawing on and respecting the cultural concepts and perspectives the language/s reflect, is privileging the voices and stories of those choosing to participate. It is not, quite simply, terra nullius–styled research. Consequently, a key task was to develop and use an accessible Aboriginal research vernacular, and infuse it into the research process. Three genres of English – Standard Australian English (SAE), Aboriginal English (AbE) and Academic English (AE) – were identified and used to facilitate the research (Daniels-Mayes, 2016). There are many possible examples to illustrate how this was achieved in my research; however, due to word limits, I will provide some select examples to illustrate the process undertaken.

In researching Aboriginal women's perceptions and experiences of health and health services, Fredericks (2008, p. 18) writes of being 'asked to "talk up" – throw my ideas out, let the women in the community hear what I was thinking and let them question me about what I was thinking about doing'. Similarly, in my research I would be asked to 'come and yarn', which included talking about me, them, the project, and life in general. Yarning is an Aboriginal cultural form of conversation 'through which both the researcher and participant journey together, visiting places and topics of interest relevant to the research' (Bessarab & Ng'andu, 2010, p. 39). Different rules or protocols, techniques and purposes exist for the carrying out and maintaining of the discussion, depending on the knowledge being sought. It involves deep discussion about a particular issue (Adams & Faulkhead, 2012; Bessarab & Ng'andu, 2010) and has been described as 'a transactional activity that involves negotiation and trust' (Imtoual, Kameniar & Bradley, 2009, p. 27). Moreover, yarning is 'a process that requires the researcher to develop and build a relationship that is accountable to Indigenous people participating in the research' (Bessarab & Ng'andu, 2010, p. 38).

This method of yarning was partnered with that of Indigenous Storywork developed by Jo-ann Archibald from the Sto:lo Nation of British Columbia, Canada. I was introduced to this Indigenous method while visiting Canada in 2014 and found it to have similarities to yarning described above. Archibald (2001, p. 1) explains that stories capture our attention and ask us 'to think deeply and to reflect upon our actions and reaction' – a process called 'Storywork'. In Archibald's methodological framework, the 4Rs of respect, responsibility, reverence and reciprocity relate to ways of working with people and with Indigenous knowledges; the remaining principles of holism, interrelatedness and synergy refer to how Indigenous knowledges and Indigenous stories are used in the research process (Archibald, 2008). It is a framework for understanding the characteristics of stories, which includes appreciating the process of storytelling, establishing a receptive learning context, and engaging in holistic meaning making (Archibald, 2008).

Together, the principles of these two Indigenous storying methods provided the guiding framework for undertaking the research. Skilful and respectful questioning and active listening are key tools in these storying methods. Active listening forces people to listen responsively to what is being shared. 'It avoids misunderstandings, as people have to confirm that they do really understand what another person has said rather than assuming that they have got it' (Daniels-Mayes, 2016, p. 80). Language barriers need to be worked through by rewording, restructuring, retelling and, at times, telling another story to clarify the point being conveyed. Such a process required me to shift between 'Englishes', from academic to everyday to Aboriginal English and back.

One significant way in which I traversed the three Englishes was through the use of metaphor and imagery located within the participants' worlds. The use of metaphor in Indigenous research is prominent (see, for example, Archibald, 2008; Kovach, 2009; Martin, 2008; Wilson, 2008).

Metaphor is a visual story (Martin, 2008) that compares two unlike objects, concepts or feelings, to establish mutual understanding. The visual story provided through metaphor enables 'listeners to walk inside the story to find their own teachings' (Kovach, 2009, p. 63). I repeatedly used metaphor in the research, particularly when working with participants to learn and build knowledge of new or complex ideas. The following story, from my research, is illustrative of this point:

> **Lesson learned today.** I gave Uncle 'Pedro' the transcript of his interview today, printed out as he doesn't like computers. An hour later I asked him what he thought. Put simply he didn't like it.
>
> I recall holding my breath and asking, 'Tell me more?' Uncle Pedro responded that reading it he 'sounded like an idiot'. Through skilful questioning and careful listening I learned he didn't believe he spoke 'like that, with the "ums" and "ahs"'. We yarned further, and I used the following metaphor to teach Uncle Pedro about raw data:
>
> Sheelagh: OK, let's think of raw data as a pumpkin you buy in the shops. You wouldn't eat it off the shelf? You'd take it home; peel it; bake it; steam it; mash it; you might add some herbs and spice or just salt?
>
> Uncle Pedro: Salt and butter?
>
> Sheelagh: Yeah, sounds good. So, this transcript is like the raw pumpkin; doesn't taste too good right now. But what I do now, with your help, is prepare it and spice it up. Take out the 'ums' and 'ahs'. Come back to you for regular tastings until it tastes good?
>
> Uncle Pedro: OK. But do I really sound like that?
>
> Sheelagh: Yeah, most of us do. Let me show you the transcript of another participant, a whitefella teacher.
>
> Uncle Pedro: (after reading through a couple of paragraphs) He's gonna need some serious spicing up. (Field notes: 25 November 2014)

In this encounter, Uncle Pedro went from being a reluctant participant, ready to withdraw, to one willing to participate and assist in the future development of the investigation. Additionally, Uncle Pedro learned a new language, Academic English. Moreover, through this transactional activity, I became the student (re)learning the power of words to both wound and heal, to both exclude and empower. My 'lesson learned' was one of many enactments of Critical Praxis Research.

It is important to note that I did not just extend this courtesy to Aboriginal participants in my research, but to all participants, understanding that they knew the meanings of the stories being shared (knowers), and therefore what was to be learned from them. At times, some 'spicing up' was involved in the writing up of the stories to avoid participants being portrayed as, for example, 'idiots', as was Uncle Pedro's initial interpretation of the raw data (Daniels-Mayes, 2016). I stress that proper ways of working through accessible language is not about compliance or manipulation. But rather it is a matter of having the consideration to attend to how access to privileged, or knowers' knowledge, often hidden in unfamiliar language, can be achieved.

Participant selection

My preference was not to predetermine the characteristics of participant teachers nor to devise a checklist against which to assess. Instead, I relied on a community nomination process (Foster, 1994; Ladson-Billings, 1994; McDonald, 1993). Here the researcher relies on community members to judge people, places and things within their own setting (McDonald, 2003). Researchers such as Delpit (1995) and Foster (1994) have written of the dangers of defining successful or good teaching without accounting for the emic (or insider) perspective. The insider is the knower of whom or what is valued by the community the teachers are intended to serve and benefit. With this in mind, my research design recognised and privileged Aboriginal students, parents and community leaders as insiders, or knowers, in their own education. Additionally, my research design recognised the experience and knowledge of key school stakeholders such as the principal, fellow teachers and, significantly, staff and visitors of the Nunga Room (a culturally safe space in the school).

Over a period of several months, interviewing referred to by Burgess (1988) as 'conversations with a purpose', which lasted from three minutes to several hours, were used. These purposeful conversations are a 'non-standardised interview [which] does not include identical questions for all those interviewed with the result that information cannot be summarised in a statistical form' (Burges, 1988, p. 138). After fulfilling my relational responsibilities by providing a brief 'who am I' and 'what am I doing here', I asked my core question: 'Who do you think is a successful teacher at this school?' or, to put it another way, 'Which teachers are doing good with our [Aboriginal] kids?' (Daniels-Mayes, 2016, p. 93). These purposeful conversations were undertaken with individuals or small groups as opportunities arose. Such moments occurred, for example, at community events, while walking down a corridor, at a staff meeting, at a football match, or in the Nunga Room.

When a name was provided, I would simply nudge for more information by asking questions like: 'How come Mr/Mrs ...?' Or, 'What does Mr/Mrs do to get nominated?' Overall, nominations were based on a variety of elements including those characteristics that matched with the international and national literature reviewed: student academic performance, high attendance rates, participation in the lesson and a high willingness to get homework completed on time. Most common though were the positive stories individuals shared with me about the caring, passionate and determined nature of the teacher with regards to the student. Also disclosed to me were classroom placement requests with particular teachers by students, parents/ caregivers and Aboriginal Education Team (AET) staff, based on the positive educational outcomes of Aboriginal students in their specific classrooms. In short, participants were the 'knowers' and I was the student learning, or as I became known, a 'stickybeak' (Aunty Nangala) sticking my nose into others' business or knowledge or lived experience so as to learn.

Am I an insider or outsider?

Many reading this chapter might assume that as an Aboriginal person, I might have the insider track on undertaking Aboriginal-centred research – that being Aboriginal myself means that I have easy access to participants and their communities, know the relevant protocols and speak the same language. But such assertions assume a homogeneity that is far from the reality of the diversity and complexity that characterises Indigenous peoples' lives around the world. There is, quite simply, no pan-Aboriginal identity in Australia. Nor do such suppositions take into consideration the influence that age, class, gender, education and ability – among a myriad of other variables – might have upon the research relationship.

Studies by researchers who had initially considered themselves to be insiders speak to this problem (see, for example, Archibald, 2008; Martin, 2008; Smith, 1999). Additionally, as Smith (1999) argues, even Western-trained Indigenous researchers who are intimately involved with community members will typically employ research techniques and methodologies that will likely marginalise the community's contribution to the research. Overall, the research advises that being an Indigenous researcher does not automatically mean that research will be undertaken in a culturally responsive way when researching in or with their own community.

When considering who should conduct research in African -American communities, Tillman (2002, p. 4) advises that it is not simply a matter of saying that the researcher must be African-American, but 'Rather it is important to consider whether the researcher has the cultural knowledge to accurately interpret and validate the experiences of African-Americans within the context of the phenomenon under study'. Similarly, Rigney (2006, p. 42) advises that 'Indigenist research principles can be drawn upon by non-Indigenous researchers who uphold its principles for Indigenous self-determination'. So, instead of the focus being on insider and outsider, Narayan (1993, p. 672) proposes:

> What we must focus our attention on is the quality of relations with the people we seek to represent in our texts: are they viewed as mere fodder for professionally self-serving statements about a generalised Other, or are they accepted as subjects with voices, views, and dilemmas – people to whom we are bonded through ties of reciprocity ...?

Consequently, as an Indigenous/Aboriginal/Kamilaroi researcher, I did not expect to be bestowed with automatic 'insider' status; quite simply, I was not. I belong to a freshwater language group, far distant from the

Aboriginal Country my research was located in or, in some cases, to the Countries of my participants and their communities. Additionally, my age, gender, class, education and ability, among other things, significantly influenced my insider or outsider status. Moreover, I was 'marked' by the community as an outsider simply by being affiliated with a university: to whom am I accountable – the university or the community – when it comes to, for example, ethics or methodology?

I am bonded to my culture and I am therefore expected by Aboriginal communities to undertake research in 'proper ways' (Aunty Nangala), adhering to cultural Aboriginal ways of knowing, being and doing relevant to the community with whom I am engaging (Daniels-Mayes & Sehlin MacNeil, 2019). I am expected to work respectfully, reciprocally and relationally, observing the dynamics of kinship structures present in the participating community. This, I found, creates a community–university tension that needs constant negotiation with community, with my PhD supervisors, and with the protocols of the academy itself, a discussion of which goes beyond the scope of this chapter. Quite simply, through my research practice I seek to become an invited and accepted insider by doing research 'proper ways'.

Conclusion

In this chapter I have applied the method of Critical Praxis Research (Kress, 2011) to problematise the question: when do I know not to know and therefore become the student and not the researcher? My aim has been to highlight the need for research to be led by the community in which the research is to be undertaken. It has been shown that this approach to research is oppositional to terra nullius–styled research that understands participants as objects of curiosity and subjects of research. So while all research should strive to centre the participant as 'knower', it is arguably more significant to do so when undertaking research in Aboriginal spaces due to the legacy of dispossessing colonisation where Aboriginal peoples were to be seen but not asked, heard, nor respected, let alone lead research.

References

Adams, K. & Faulkhead, S. (2012). This is not a guide to indigenous research partnerships: But it could help. *Information, Communication and Society*, *15*(7), pp. 1016–1036.

Archibald, A. (2008). *Indigenous storywork: Educating the heart, mind, body, and spirit*. Vancouver: UBC Press.

Archibald, J. A. (2001). Editorial: sharing Aboriginal knowledge and Aboriginal ways of knowing. *Canadian Journal of Native Education*, *25*(1), pp. 1–5.

Australian Institute for Aboriginal and Torres Strait Islander Studies (2012). *Guidelines for ethical research in Australian Indigenous studies*. https://bit.ly/3kTXXMS.

Berryman, M., SooHoo, S. & Nevin, A. (Eds.) (2013). *Culturally responsive methodologies*. London: Emerald Group Publishing.

Bessarab, D. & Ng'andu, B. (2010). Yarning about yarning as a legitimate method in Indigenous research. *International Journal of Critical Indigenous Studies*, *3*(1), pp. 37–50.

Bishop, R. (2011). *Freeing ourselves*. Rotterdam: Sense Publishers.

Bourke, E. (1999). Dilemmas of integrity and knowledge: Protocol in Aboriginal research. In School of Indigenous Australian Studies, *Indigenous research ethics: Papers from the conference held in Townsville in September 1995*, pp. 9–20. Centre for Social and Welfare Research: James Cook University, Townsville, 1999.

Brayboy, B. M. J. & Maughan, E. (2009). Indigenous knowledges and the story of the bean. *Harvard Educational Review*, *79*(1), pp. 1–21.

Burgess, R. G. (1988). Conversations with a purpose: The ethnographic interview in educational research. *Studies in Qualitative Methodology: Conducting Qualitative Research*, *1*(1), pp. 137–155.

Carlson, B. (2013). The new frontier: Emergent Indigenous identities and social media. In Harris, M., Nakata, M. & Carlson, B. (Eds.), *The politics of identity: Emerging Indigeneity*, pp. 147–168. Sydney: University of Technology Sydney E-Press.

Castagno, A. E. (2006). *Uncertain but always unthreatening: Multicultural education in two urban middle schools* (unpublished dissertation). University of Wisconsin, Madison.

Castagno, A. E. & Brayboy, B. M. J. (2008). Culturally responsive schooling for Indigenous youth: A review of the literature. *Review of Educational Research*, *78*(4), pp. 941–993.

Daniels-Mayes, S. (2016). *Culturally responsive pedagogies of success: Improving educational outcomes for Aboriginal students* (unpublished doctoral thesis). University of South Australia, Adelaide.

Daniels-Mayes, S. & Sehlin MacNiel, K. (2019). Indigenous diplomacy as an act of self-determination: Resisting assimilationist research practices in Australian Aboriginal and Sami in Sweden contexts. *Whitehead Journal of Diplomacy and International Relations, 21*(1), pp. 36–53.

Delpit, L. (1995). *Other people's children: Cultural conflict in the classroom.* New York: New Press.

Flinders University (n.d.) Appropriate terminology, Indigenous Australian peoples, module 7, https://bit.ly/3tW4iKX.

Foster, M. (1994). Effective Black teachers: A literature review. In E. Hollins, J. King, and W. Hayman (Eds). *Teaching diverse populations: Formulating a knowledge base*, pp. 207–225. Albany: State University of New York Press.

Fredericks, B. (2007). Utilising the concept of pathways as a framework of Indigenous research. *Australian Journal of Indigenous Research, 36*, supplement, pp. 15–24.

Gay, G. (2010). *Culturally responsive teaching: Theory, research, and practice*, 2nd edition. New York: Teachers College Press.

Gower, G. C. (2012). Ethical research in Indigenous Australian contexts and its practical implementation. In *Proceedings of Innovative research in a changing and challenging world*, pp. 47–58. Phuket, Thailand: Australian Multicultural Interaction Institute.

Hart, V. & Whatman, S. (1998). Decolonising the concept of knowledge. Paper presented at the HERDSA conference, Auckland, 7–10 July.

Imtoual, A., Kameniar, B., & Bradley, D. (2009). Bottling the good stuff: Stories of hospitality and yarnin' in a multi-racial kindergarten. *Australasian Journal of Early Childhood, 34*(2), pp. 24–30.

Kovach, M. (2009). *Indigenous methodologies: Characteristics, conversations and contexts.* Toronto: University of Toronto Press.

Kress, T. M. (2011). *Critical praxis research: Breathing new life into research methods for teachers.* Dordrecht: Springer Netherlands.

Ladson-Billings, G. (1994). *The dreamkeepers: Successful teachers of African American children.* San Francisco: Jossey-Bass.

Lynn, M., Yosso, T. J., Solórzano, D. G. & Parker, L. (2002). Critical race theory and education: Qualitative research in the new millennium. *Qualitative Inquiry, 8*(3), pp. 3–6.

Martin, K. (2008). The intersection of Aboriginal knowledges, Aboriginal literacies, and new learning pedagogy for Aboriginal students. In A. Healy

(Ed.), *Multiliteracies and diversity in education: New pedagogies for expanding landscapes*, pp. 58–80. Melbourne: Oxford University Press.

Martin, K. (2003). Ways of knowing, being and doing: A theoretical framework and methods for Indigenous and Indigenist research. *Journal of Australian Studies, 27*(76), pp. 203–214.

Mathews, C. (2012). Maths is storytelling: Maths is beautiful. In K. Price (Ed.), *Aboriginal and Torres Strait Islander education: An introduction for the teaching profession*, pp. 108–134. Port Melbourne: Cambridge University Press.

Mcdonald, H. (2003). Exploring possibilities through critical race theory: Exemplary pedagogical practices for Indigenous students. Refereed paper presented at NZARE/AARE joint conference, Auckland, New Zealand.

Moreton-Robinson, A. M. (2011). Performing white possession: Bodies that matter at the beach. In P. Power (Ed.) *Border, theory, art and power*. London: Lang Publishing.

Moreton-Robinson, A. (2000). *Talkin' up to the white woman: Indigenous women and feminism*. St Lucia: University of Queensland Press.

Narayan, K. (1993). How native is a 'native' anthropologist? *American Anthropologist, 95*(3) (new series), pp. 671–686.

Rigney, L-I. (2006). 'Indigenous Australian views on knowledge production and Indigenist research'. In J.E. Kunnie & N.I. Goduka (Eds.), *Indigenous peoples' wisdom and power: Affirming our knowledge through narrative*, pp. 32–50. Farnham, UK: Ashgate Publishing.

Smith, L-T. (1999). *Decolonising methodologies: Research and Indigenous people*. London and New York: Zed Books.

Tillman, L. C. (2002). Culturally sensitive research approaches: An African-American perspective. *Educational Researcher, 31*, 9, pp. 3–12.

Wilson, S. (2001). What is an Indigenous research methodology? *Canadian Journal of Native Education, 25*(2), pp. 175–179.

Wilson, S. (2008). *Research is ceremony*. Black Point, Nova Scotia: Fernwood Publishing.

Yunkaporta, T. & Kirby, M. (2011). Yarning up Indigenous pedagogies: A dialogue about eight Aboriginal ways of learning. In R. Bell, G. Milgate & N. Purdie (Eds.), *Two way teaching and learning: Toward culturally reflective and relevant education*, pp. 146–52. Camberwell, VIC: ACER Press.

8
Trepidation, trust and time: working with Aboriginal communities

Julie Welsh and Cathie Burgess

Aboriginal people are understandably suspicious and reticent about universities and academics conducting research in their communities given the history of disrespectful, misconceived and often divisive research studies that have caused more harm than good (Daniels-Mayes, this volume; Martin, 2008; Rigney, 1999; Riley, this volume). As Dodson (2003) clearly notes: 'Since their first intrusive gaze, colonising cultures have had a preoccupation with observing, analysing, studying, classifying and labelling Aborigines and Aboriginality. Under that gaze, Aboriginality changed from being daily practice to 'being a problem to be solved' (p. 27). The notion of Aboriginal people as 'a problem to be solved' still unpins many government policies and strategies (Buxton, 2017), and, usually, the broader community's perceptions of Aboriginal peoples.

Researcher propensity to objectify Indigenous peoples, position 'them' through deficit assumptions and question the validity of Indigenous knowledges, values, beliefs and practices (Osborne, 2018) has resulted in a number of Indigenous researchers (see for instance, Martin, 2008; Moreton-Robinson, 2013; Rigney, 1999; Tuhawai Smith,

J. Welsh & C. Burgess (2021). Trepidation, trust and time: Working with Aboriginal communities. In V. Rawlings, J. Flexner & L. Riley (Eds.), *Community-Led Research: Walking new pathways together.* Sydney: Sydney University Press.

2012) calling for clear ethical protocols and practices for researching in Indigenous communities. This must include acknowledging Indigenous standpoints and applying critical Indigenous research methodologies in collaboration with the Indigenous peoples and communities. As Osborne (2018) notes, researchers need to articulate and work 'from knowledges and lived realities generated outside the locus of institutional power which tended to be the domain of powerful white men' (p. 27). Osborne 2018, p. 27) also identifies issues such as power, culture, values and language that need to be attended to, and that privileging Aboriginal voices through personal and collective narratives recognises the centrality of Aboriginal communication traditions. Researchers need to be aware that 'The term "research" is inextricably linked to European imperialism and colonialism. The word itself, "research" is probably one of the dirtiest words in the indigenous world's vocabulary' (Smith, 1999, p. 1). This reminds us of an extensive history of Eurocentric bias, prejudice and, consequently, ill-informed findings.

This chapter outlines key issues for Aboriginal community members and researchers when planning and conducting research that is meaningful, important and beneficial for community. It draws on a yarning circle led by two local Aboriginal community members (Mary and Bryan[1]) consisting of researchers, community workers and others from diverse backgrounds working in this area. The yarning circle leaders led a discussion about researching in Aboriginal communities by articulating how they perceive and conduct Community-Led Research (CLR). Moreover, this chapter is constructed in a way that not only articulates the key issues involved but demonstrates how these are enacted through foregrounding personal and professional positioning, unpacking the notion of community and highlighting the key tenets of ethical and respectful work in this space. Finally, we identify ways in which this work 'bumps up against' the institutions and cultures within which we work as researchers.

In order to contextualise our work, we offer the following description of the Aboriginal community we live and work in.

---

1   Pseudonyms for local Aboriginal community members leading the yarning circle.

As Aboriginal and non-Aboriginal researchers and educators working in our local Aboriginal community, we carry with us a deep-seated awareness of colonisation and the intergenerational trauma associated with this. We do not assume or apply this to the people we engage with unless they choose to share this and give their express permission. This further indicates the diversity, complexities and nuances that exist in our community of Redfern, an urban centre at the first point of invasion and in which a unique and resilient community has grown despite ongoing oppression through the institutional and broader society structures that underpin settler colonies such as Australia (Buxton, 2017; Dodson, 2003). Here, Aboriginal people have carved out a significant heritage, culture and presence that reverberates in Aboriginal communities across Australia, and constantly reminds non-Indigenous Australia that Aboriginal peoples and cultures are alive and thriving. In saying that, we are acutely aware how this can create conflicting agendas and politics and so negotiate this terrain carefully and respectfully.

Individual and collective positioning

Positioning ourselves in research contexts is important in two key ways: recognising how it operates within the power dynamics of a research setting (Howard & Rawsthorne, this volume), and how the participants engage subject positions as a resource to narratively construct their identity (Soriede, 2006, p. 527) within this context. As Aboriginal co-researchers and participants are often positioned as 'other', foregrounding their lived experiences through narrative traditions such as yarning, storying and humorous anecdotes provides opportunities to destabilise and decentre assumptions and knowledge 'truths'.

Researcher awareness of their biases and assumptions is central to positionality and requires ongoing reflexivity to challenge and problematise the social and structural issues that marginalise and deny Aboriginal peoples' histories and cultures (Russell-Mundine, 2012). As Moreton-Robinson (2003, p. 66) notes, 'whiteness is both the measure and the marker of normality in Australian society, yet remains invisible for most white women and men, they do not associate it with conferring dominance and privilege'. D'Antoine, et al. (2019, p. 3) suggest that critical reflection is essential throughout the research process and acknowledgement of insider/outsider positioning critical to rigour in qualitative research. They note that researchers can occupy various insider and outsider positions at different times and in different ways, and so avoiding assumptions, expectations and complacency is important in developing respectful, trusting and reciprocal relationships. As Russell-Mundine (2012, p. 86) demonstrates: 'I have, hopefully, developed a greater capacity to question my own culture, my whiteness and the structures and privileges that the dominant culture has created'.

For non-Indigenous researchers, Delpit (1993) suggests that deep listening is required as a member of the dominant (and harming) culture where:

> [to] put our beliefs on hold is to cease to exist as ourselves for a moment – and that is not easy … because it means turning yourself inside out, giving up your own sense of who you are, and being willing to see yourself in the unflattering light of another's angry gaze … it is the only way to learn what it might feel like to be someone else and the only way to start a dialogue. (p. 139)

These ideas indicate the complexity and emotional labour involved in ethical research with marginalised communities, in order to attend to difficult knowledges and uncomfortable 'truths' (McMahon & McKnight, this volume). These difficult knowledges are often revealed in the research process as Aboriginal narratives can be interwoven with lived experiences of trauma and tragedy. For the non-Indigenous person new to these experiences, Simon (2011, p. 434) suggests that 'difficulty happens when one's conceptual framework, emotional attachments and conscious and unconscious desires delimit one's ability to settle meaning in past events'. Here, Simon recognises that many non-Indigenous people are unaware of the tragic circumstances for many victims of oppression, and when confronted with the reality of this, struggle to reconcile this with their understanding of their own culture and history. For some, this renders identity precarious and uncertain, invoking feelings of vulnerability (Harrison, Burke & Clarke, 2018). By embracing respectful and reciprocal relationships with community members/researchers, a sense of agency can be restored, and valuable partnerships formed (Howard & Rawsthorne, this volume).

Introducing and positioning the researchers

We, the authors of this chapter, are Aboriginal and non-Aboriginal parents, educators, community members and researchers.

> My name is Julie Welsh, I'm a Gamilaroi Murawarri woman, originally from Gunnedah, New South Wales, I grew up as very much a part of the Redfern community, from about the age of five when Mum and Dad brought us all down to Sydney. I'd like to pay my respects and acknowledge the traditional owners of the lands that we are meeting on, the Gadigal people of the Eora Nation. I would also like to pay respects to Elders both past and present and acknowledge those Aboriginal people who are in this room, and everybody coming together and making a real effort to create this space so that we can have a yarn. I work for local government and my role as a Community Development Officer is to support cultural and community programs to meet the needs and wants of local communities.

> My name is Cathie Burgess and I am a non-Aboriginal teacher who has worked in Aboriginal education for over 35 years, currently as a lecturer/researcher at an elite university. I was born on and therefore also acknowledge Gadigal Country and that Aboriginal sovereignty was never ceded. I am a parent of Aboriginal children and we are all involved in local Aboriginal community sports and organisations. While I have a personal and professional passion and commitment to Aboriginal education, I am aware of my white privilege and the cultural biases that accompany insider/outsider positioning. Thus, I am guided by Aboriginal family, colleagues and friends in this lifelong learning journey that never ceases to surprise and reward.

In order to better understand this positioning, we unpack what we mean by community, since this concept is at the centre of a conceptual understanding of CLR.

(Re)defining community

The term 'community' is frequently applied to Aboriginal contexts, with little explanation as to what this actually means conceptually and/ or in practice. Certainly, it moves beyond common or normative understandings of the term due largely to the complex, localised and nuanced historical, cultural, social and political experiences of Aboriginal and Torres Strait Islander peoples as an oppressed 'other' in a settler colony, as Ted Wilkes, a Nyungar researcher from Western Australia, notes (Dudgeon, et al., 2014, p. 6):

> The Aboriginal community can be interpreted as geographical, social and political. It places Aboriginal people as part of, but different from, the rest of Australian society. Aboriginal people identify themselves with the idea of being part of 'community'; it gives us a sense of unity and strength.

This description by Bryan alerts us to the importance of local community:

> Redfern is all about trailblazers from Redfern. This used to be the capital for self-determination and civil rights movements, a hub for Aboriginal people and many different communities coming here to connect, especially Stolen Generation[2] and people who are looking for work. Over the years, most recently, Redfern has changed a lot. Unfortunately, many of our people have been moved out of the area, so we're trying to recapture that spirit and culture back into the area so that there's always going to be

---

2   The Stolen Generation are Aboriginal people who were removed from their families as children and put in institutions to assimilate them into white society to provide cheap domestic and farm labour.

a reason for Aboriginal people to come back and connect with Redfern.

Mary further notes the impact of changing demographics in the area, an issue faced by many urban communities that were once considered 'slums' by outsiders:

Dealing with gentrification is our reality in this area, you know? So, as a community, and a wider community, how do we deal with that? It's terrible for families to be moved out, it's terrible for our Elders and other senior people to be moved out and put somewhere else when this is the only place that they've known for 40–50 years ... Redfern is such a significant place for us, and where I'm situated right now, I work right next to the Block.[3] For me, that gives me energy every day. It's a challenge right now because it's under construction but in 12 months' time, there should be Aboriginal families back on the block, that's where our families belong.

Ethical and respectful work

In response to the colonising practices of Western research, Indigenous people and organisations have developed and implemented ethical and respectful protocols for working *with* Aboriginal communities rather than *about* or *to* Aboriginal communities (Dreise & Mazurski, 2018, p. 10). In Australia, key university and other research institutions ethics procedures are influenced by documents produced by the Australian Institute of Aboriginal and Torres Strait Islander Studies and the National Health and Medical Research Council. The Lowitja Institute (2011) also published a comprehensive, practical guide for researchers detailing how the six principles of ethical Indigenous research – spirit

---

3   The 'Block' is the local name for an area of Redfern owned by the Aboriginal Housing Company that used to have a large number of Aboriginal families living there. This is currently being redeveloped to include university student accommodation as well as affordable housing for Aboriginal people.

and integrity, reciprocity, respect, equality, survival and protection and responsibility – can be actioned. Critical ethical questions raised are, 'who controls the research process?', 'who does the research benefit?' and 'who owns the new knowledge?' (p. 24).

Crucial to planning and designing research is support for community priorities, time for community consultation, two-way co-researching in a collaborative learning partnership and audience-appropriate translation and dissemination of research findings (D'Antoine et al., 2019). Certainly, one of the main complaints from Aboriginal communities is that researchers arrive, often unannounced, with a predefined research plan, expecting the community to 'rubber-stamp' their plan. Mary identifies a similar context where Aboriginal protocols are ignored:

> [W]e certainly know when it's assessment time, because you have uni students coming into community wanting to speak to Aboriginal people as if we're here waiting for them to tick their boxes. These fullas bring their privilege and sense of entitlement thinking they can come into community and just take, not follow protocols, not show respect, not engage with community proper way, but simply take, this is ignorance at its best!

This indicates that following community protocols, building relationships and trust needs to occur before the research design is finalised. It is important to ascertain if the proposed research supports community priorities, privileges community voices, respects community views on data/knowledge, ownership/copyright and contributes new knowledge that acknowledges and augments community cultural strength.

In working with Nyoongar people in south-east Western Australia, Wright, Lin and O'Connell (2016, p. 91) identified humility, inquisitiveness and openness as key attributes for working in Aboriginal contexts. Humility involves a willingness to learn from and understand Aboriginal co-researchers, 'to find out what makes us Nyoongars tick in the first instance ...' Researchers' readiness to admit their lack of knowledge and mistakes is an important signifier of cultural humility. Inquisitiveness was noted through the effect of shared

Elder life stories, which were at times traumatic and uncomfortable for researchers, but resulted in a transformational understanding of the issues, concerns and resilience of Aboriginal peoples. As a deeper relationship emerges, Wright, Lin and O'Connell (2016) note that the experiential learning inherent in the research process created researcher openness to new knowledges, understandings and ways of doing things, which was critical for an overall shift in how to work with Aboriginal people to meet their needs.

'You call that research, we say protocol'

In a departure from the commonly held idea that research is the arena of universities and academics, working honestly with Aboriginal communities requires alternative conceptualisations and approaches to what research means outside the academy, as the title of this chapter and Mary's observations imply:

> I've got to go and actually seek advice on that within community. And that might not necessarily be one conversation. That could probably be three or four conversations over a period of time. So if you come in and say that you want the answer within the next couple hours or even days, that probably won't happen.

Indeed, over the past 20 or so years, there have been purposeful moves towards research methodologies that recognise the complexity of diverse Aboriginal worldviews, lived experiences and the effects of marginalisation and therefore call for a critical rethinking of positivist approaches and Western 'truths'. As Henry et al. (2002, p. 2) note, methodology is 'neither value-free nor culturally pure abstraction', so researcher positionality and the research methods they choose is a significant consideration when conducting research with Aboriginal people. Rigney (1999, p. 632), for instance, argues that 'Indigenous peoples must now be involved in defining, controlling and owning epistemology and ontologies that value and legitimate the Indigenous experiences'. This founding principle of Critical Indigenous Methodologies (see Martin, 2008; Rigney, 1999; Tuhawai Smith, 2012) is designed to counteract the oppressive, often harmful practices of Western research. These researchers also privilege Indigenous epistemologies, ontologies, axiologies and methodologies as relational, holistic, culturally located, politically aware, respectful, reciprocal and cognisant of discourse. Smith (1999, p. 193) suggests that when Indigenous people become researchers, 'questions are framed differently, priorities are ranked differently, problems are defined differently; and people participate on different terms'.

Co-produced research

In efforts to be more culturally respectful and politically active, researchers could engage with their communities through co-producing research. For instance, Banks, Hart, Pahl & Ward (2019, p. 5) suggest that:

> Co-production refers as much to the spirit and philosophy of the research as it does the mechanics of doing it, [and a] conscious awareness of on the part of all co-researchers [that] people come to the research from different positions of status, power, wealth, ability and confidence.

Notably, co-production is relative to context, consciously employing expertise in empowering and respectful ways to focus on the production of knowledge for social change rather than social change itself as an outcome. This then suggests that research methodologies such as participatory action research where the processes and ongoing knowledge (re)creation are the focus, tend to be conducive to a co-production approach. These research practices are well suited to Indigenous contexts not only for their obvious goal of active participation, but also for their community-based analysis of social problems, co-production of knowledge, which opens up space for Aboriginal epistemologies and ontologies, as well as community-driven action for change (Henry et al. 2002, p. 8). Mary describes a contextual example where the local Redfern Aboriginal community takes back control of their flag-raising ceremony from a government organisation:

[W]e talk about community development, we're very strong on that – everything is community-driven and about empowering our community. It might be just this little ceremony that you think, 'What's the big deal?' But symbolism is everything and seeing community say, 'No, this is how we're going to do this. We're going to have it at one of our black organisations, we're going to raise the Aboriginal flag, and that's the start of our celebrations for the week.' Within that comes those particular ceremonies that will take place, we're reclaiming our ways of doing. This is what community decision making is all about.

This comment describes the importance of community-conceptualised and driven action that speaks to the heart of what CLR might mean.

Emerging here is the importance of positioning community member's front and centre of the CLR process. This includes identifying the research problem, co-designing the process, negotiating data ownership, and disseminating the findings. As Clapham (2011) asserts, 'research which is most highly valued by Aboriginal communities is community-controlled and asset- [or strengths] based, and that leadership at both community and academic levels is critical for such research to succeed'. Moreover, the research needs to emerge from listening and dialogue, capture the diversity of experiences, build the capacity of all involved, and benefit the community as well as be accountable to the community (Terarre & Rawsthorne, 2019, p. 145). Bryan comments on the importance of Elder engagement in this process:

[T]he most inspiring thing was that we had Elders coming in to engage in our community meetings and discussions, which was completely organic. That's because they understand what we're trying to do, and they're trying to show that support to us as well.

For Aboriginal community members and researchers, accountability to community is paramount and there are immediate consequences for not following protocols that impact on everyday lives that are generally not evident to non-Indigenous researchers. Mary explains:

And we know straight up that if we do something wrong, or we didn't consult properly or we thought we were real deadly and were going to make a decision on something, we get ripped straight away. We get told straight up. I could get that phone call at 10 o'clock at night, so it's not a 9 to 5 thing. Community is always community; and we are always accountable.

These critical methodological approaches contribute to the bigger picture of decolonising research which seeks to privilege Aboriginal voices and acknowledge their agency in producing as well as critiquing research processes and outputs. This includes problematising and changing institutional and policy structures that undermine, silence and/or sideline Aboriginal voices (D'Antione et al. 2019, pp. 2–3). Moreover, this strength-based approach is enriched when researchers commit to deep ongoing reflexivity to ensure an awareness of the influence of their positionality on research processes.

Circumlocutive yarning

We're kind of hoping that it's more of a yarn, as opposed to a formal presentation, because we're trying to do those practices that we do when we come together where we sit around and we yarn, that's what's really important. It doesn't take away the importance of what the conversations are, but these are the ways we do things. So, we see this as equality of everybody sitting around and coming together. (Mary)

In the Australian context, yarning is becoming an increasingly recognisable form of communication and data generation in Indigenous research methodologies, respecting that participants are often marginalised and/or voiceless (Besserab & Ng'andu, 2010; Laycock, Walker, Harrison & Brands, 2011; Shay, 2019; Terarre & Rawsthorne, 2019). Bessarab and Ng'andu (2010, p. 37) describe yarning as 'an Indigenous cultural form of conversation' that asks questions such as 'where you from?' and 'who's your mob?' to indicate kinship, Country and community ties, and develop and/or strengthen connections based on this information. Locating each other within our meaning systems (Martin, 2003) in order to understand and negotiate boundaries and protocols, supports the development of genuine relationships before the research begins (Shay, 2019). Yarning circles encourage circular rather than linear discussion, reflecting Aboriginal epistemology (Wright, Lyn & O'Connell, 2016, p. 87) and providing opportunities for participants to contextualise and contribute their personal experiences as they wish. This circumlocutive approach appears vague, oblique and deliberately avoiding the point, but it is purposively employed to assess researcher patience, perseverance and open-mindedness and draw out hidden agendas and motivations. Paradoxically, it can also be part of the relationship-building process. Researchers therefore need to be prepared for the investment of time and the difficult questions that may be asked, be flexible and adaptable to allow for possible variations and/or changes to their plans, and potentially rethink their positioning and ways of working (McMahon & McKnight, this volume). It is a priority, though, to retain trust, integrity and credibility even if it means the research project needs to be reconceptualised or abandoned.

Bessarab and Ng'andu (2010) identify four types of yarning: the social, research, collaborative and the therapeutic yarn. The social yarn is an informal conversation that can include 'gossip, news, humour, advice and whatever information both parties feel inclined to share in the moment' (p. 40), is often the foundation upon which trust is built and may determine what will be revealed or not in the research yarn (Shay, 2019). The research yarn is more formal as the research topic is the focus of the yarn; it is similar to a semi-structured interview, but often punctuated with personal, often contextual anecdotes. In the collaborative yarn, key issues and themes emerging from the research are discussed and 'unpacked' in order to visualise and articulate where the research is heading. Finally, the therapeutic yarn emerges organically if a participant reveals a traumatic or intensely personal or emotional experience, and so the researcher needs to focus on deep listening and support (not counselling). The meaning-making emerging from this can 'empower and support the participant to re-think their understanding of their experience in new and different ways' (Bessarab & Ng'andu, 2010, p. 41).

Central to the yarning process is deep listening (Laycock, Walker, Harrison & Brands, 2011, p. 201; Wallerstein, 1992), which includes silence and stillness (Terrare & Rawsthorne, 2019, p. 6). Dadirri, a Ngengiwumirri word from the Daly River area in the Northern Territory (Miriam-Rose Ungunmerr-Baumann, 1993 in Laycock, Walker, Harrison & Brands, 2011, p. 53), describes an inner, deep listening involving contemplation, observation and connectedness only available in reciprocal relationships (McMahon & McKnight, this volume). It recognises people as unique, diverse and complicated, fostering a way of learning and co-producing knowledge. It is central to the project of decolonising research, reclaiming epistemology and unpacking social, political and cultural concepts as mediated through Indigenous knowledges (Terrare & Rawsthorne, 2019, p. 7). For non-Indigenous researchers it is an opportunity to participate beyond one's comfort zone, see perspectives that a Western-oriented approach may not reveal (Bessarab & Ng'andu, 2010, p. 47), and seek a deeper understanding of the importance of a holistic and collaborative approach to research.

Conflicting systems: the reality of working in the margins

The stark contrast in the organisational, cultural, social and political constructs of universities and communities becomes a key issue for researchers working ethically and respectfully in communities, particularly in marginalised communities. The nature of academia and the way in which structures and processes are organised, render university systems inflexible and dogmatic in meeting procedural and audit requirements (Rawsthorne & de Pree, 2019). This creates significant barriers when working with local community people and/or small non-for-profit, often under-resourced organisations.

Nature of academia

Universities are generally seen as society's holders of 'important' knowledge, the places where new knowledge is discovered and shared with other knowledge holders such as governments and policy makers.

Significantly, this constructs an elitist frame that dismisses external, particularly community-generated knowledge, as meaningful to the academy (Rawsthorne & de Pree, 2019, p. 145). This attitude impacts on academics who embark upon research in their local communities as the intellectual, social and emotional labour academics invest in such projects is not recognised in workloads, promotion or publishing in non-traditional outlets not measured in university metrics (Rawsthorne & de Pree, 2019, p. 145).

Cameron et al. (2019, pp. 72–73) note that issues such as sources of knowledge, power, uncertainty, worldviews and audiences arise when universities partner with marginalised communities. Sources of knowledge from communities comprise largely of lived experiences and practices that are very different from academic sources, and ironically, these experiences are negative due to the way in which institutions and their knowledges exclude and devalue these communities. This speaks to issues of power, the uncertainty of participation and contrasting perspectives of what constitutes valuable knowledge. Rawsthorne and de Pree (2019, p. 146) suggest that community-led and co-designed research develops knowledge and practices grounded in the lived experiences of participants and therefore of value to them. If value and impact is indeed the goal of socially orientated research, then this knowledge is new, inclusive and aligns with broader society goals of social justice.

Organisational issues

University administration and organisational procedures create barriers when working with communities, and can undermine the credibility, trust and relationship-building processes all essential for working locally (Webster, Hill, Hall & See, this volume). By and large, these issues include (see also Robinson, Flexner & Miller, this volume):

- Short-term funding cycles. Community projects are time-consuming with many months invested in building relationships before the research begins.
- Project outputs are often non-traditional as maintaining the integrity and ethics of community research means producing

something of value to the community, yet funding is often contingent upon producing academic outputs.

- Reimbursing local community members for their expertise and time can be extremely complicated as human resources procedures require tax file numbers, bank accounts, a fixed address or identification such as a passport or driver's licence. When working with marginalised people, this is not always possible and so their expertise is rendered worthless by procedural/systemic exclusion and therefore reinforces the elitist and inaccessible nature of universities, despite their rhetoric of inclusion and community-mindedness.

- Universities often prefer research projects to occur on their grounds or a suitable venue, possibly to avoid external costs or to oversee community-led projects that they are funding. However, for many communities, people need to be in their 'comfort zone' to embark on a trust-building endeavour with researchers, and for Aboriginal people, this means working on Country and in the community.

- The community people we research with are accountable to their own community and this frames what they do, how they work and what emerges from the research, and as such we are bound by these imperatives regardless of where we sit within the institution. As Mary notes, 'at the end of the day we're always part of the community that we come from. And we're always accountable to them. And that's very important'.

Implications

There are a number of implications for researchers working in their local Aboriginal communities. Perhaps the most difficult but significant is developing trust in order to build relationships and authentic engagement. Pigza (2016) notes that this is 'human work that requires time, transparency, authenticity, trust, accountability, and clear communication' (p. 96). As Bryan suggests, 'everything should be an opportunity to learn and engage, whether it's Aboriginal people to non-Aboriginal people, or non-Aboriginal people to Aboriginal people. And that's about creating those times to engage with everyone'. As collaboration is critical in research with communities in order to ethically respond to local issues, how to proceed is an important consideration. For instance, should we engage in community-led, co-designed, two-way capacity building, participatory action research, or as our community members describe this, as protocols and accountability? Without investing the time needed to deconstruct these concepts in the context within which the research is to occur with the people who are central to the research, then it is unlikely to produce the desired outcomes, and the loss of trust between the researcher and community is far more detrimental than not completing the research.

If social justice and change underpins research in community contexts, in Aboriginal contexts, decolonising research methodologies are significant in creating the conditions for change. It recognises that the 'term research is inextricably linked to European imperialism and colonialism' (Denzin & Lincoln, 2014, p. 5) and that Indigenous knowledges must be privileged and listened to at deep levels. It foregrounds Aboriginal empowerment, governance and ownership throughout the process and a deep awareness by non-Indigenous participants of the history of harm and ongoing deficit discourses that have emerged from inappropriate research. It acknowledges ' Indigenous researchers and community members as experts in the research process and agents for change' (D'Antoine, 2019, p. 2) and the importance of reporting findings from a strength-based position through Aboriginal voices.

This chapter highlights key challenges for working in the margins with local communities to effect change, many of which arise from the institution rather than the community. It calls for researcher and institutional humility, flexibility and reciprocity as representatives of colonising structures and for the positioning of social justice, sovereignty and self-determination front, centre and foundation of the research process.

References

Australian Council for Educational Research (2012). *Guidelines for ethical research in Indigenous studies*. Canberra: Australian Institute of Aboriginal and Torres Strait Islander Studies.

Banks, S., Hart, A., Pahl, K. & Ward, P. (2019). *Co-producing research: A community development approach*. Bristol: Policy Press.

Baum, F. (1998). *The new public health: An Australian perspective*. Melbourne: Oxford University Press.

Buxton, L. (2017). Ditching deficit thinking: Changing to a culture of high expectations. *Issues in Educational Research, 27*(2), pp. 198–214

Bessarab, D. & Ng'andu, B. (2010). Yarning about yarning as a legitimate method in Indigenous research. *International Journal of Critical Indigenous Studies, 3*(1), pp. 37–50.

Cameron, J., Wenger-Trayner, B., Wenger-Trayner, E., Hart A., Buttery, L., Kourkoutas, E., Eryigit-Madzwamuse, S. & Rathbone, A. (2019). Community-university partnership research retreats: A productive force for developing communities of research practice. In S. Banks, A. Hart, K. Pahl & P. Ward (Eds.), *Co-producing research: A community development approach*. Bristol: Policy Press.

Clapham, K. (2011). Indigenous-led intervention research: The benefits, challenges and opportunities. *International Journal of Critical Indigenous Studies, 4*(2), pp. 40–48.

D'Antoine, H., Abbott, P., Sherwood, J., Wright, M., Dowling, C., Lehmann, D., Eades, A. & Bessarab, D. (2019). A collaborative yarn on qualitative health research with Aboriginal communities. *Australian Indigenous Health Bulletin, 19*(2).

Delpit, L. (1993). The silenced dialogue: Power and pedagogy in educating other people's children. In L. Weis & M. Fine. (Eds). *Beyond silenced voices: Class, race, and gender in United States schools*, pp. 119–144. New York: State University of New York Press.

Denzin, N. K., & Lincoln, Y. S. (2014). Introduction: Critical methodologies and Indigenous inquiry. In N. K. Denzin, Y. S. Lincoln, & L. T. Smith (Eds.), *Handbook of critical and Indigenous methodologies*, pp. 1–20. London: Sage.

Dodson, M. (2003). The end in the beginning. In M. Grossman (Ed.), *Blacklines: Contemporary critical writing by Indigenous Australians*, pp. 25–42. Melbourne: Melbourne University Press.

Drawson, A. S., Toombs, E. & Mushquash, C. J. (2017). Indigenous research methods: A systematic review. *The International Indigenous Policy Journal, 8*(2). doi: 10.18584/iipj.2017.8.2.5

Dreise, T. & Mazurski, E. (2018). *Weaving knowledges: Knowledge exchange, co-design and community-based participatory research and evaluation in Aboriginal communities*. Sydney: NSW Department of Aboriginal Affairs.

Dudgeon, P., Milroy, H. & and Walker. R. (2014). *Working together: Aboriginal and Torres Strait Islander mental health and wellbeing principles and practice*. Canberra: Commonwealth of Australia

Foley, D. (2003). Indigenous epistemology and Indigenous standpoint theory. *Social Alternatives, 22*(1), pp. 44–52.

Harrison, N., Burke, J. & Clarke, I. (2018). Stolen generations: Teaching *about* the experiences of trauma. *Knowledge Cultures* 6(2), pp. 51–63

Henry, J., Dunbar, T., Arnott, A., Scrimgeour, M., Matthews, S., Murakami-Gold. & Chamberlain, A. (2002). Indigenous research reform agenda: Rethinking research methodologies. *Links Monograph Series 2*. Canberra: Cooperative Research Centre for Aboriginal & Tropical Health, The Lowitja Institute.

Laycock, A. with Walker, D., Harrison, N. & Brands, J. (2011). *Researching Indigenous health: A practical guide for researchers*. Melbourne: The Lowitja Institute.

Martin, K. (2003). Ways of knowing, being and doing: A theoretical framework and methods for Indigenous and Indigenist re-search. *Journal of Australian Studies, 27*(76), pp. 203–214.

Martin, K. (2008). *Please knock before you enter: Aboriginal regulation of outsiders and the implications for researchers*. Tenerfiffi, QLD: Southern Cross University.

Moreton-Robinson, A. (2003). Tiddas talkin' up to the white woman: When Huggins et al. took on Bell. In M. Grossman (Ed.), *Blacklines: Contemporary critical writing by Indigenous Australians*, pp. 66–77. Melbourne, Australia: Melbourne University Press.

Moreton-Robinson, A. (2013). Towards an Australian Indigenous women's standpoint theory. *Australian Feminist Studies, 28*(78), pp. 331–347.

Nakata, M. (2007a). The cultural interface. *The Australian Journal of Indigenous Education, 36*(S1), pp. 7–14.

National Health and Medical Research Council (2018). *Ethical conduct in research with Aboriginal and Torres Strait Islander Peoples and communities: Guidelines for researchers and stakeholders*. Canberra: NHMRC.

Osborne, S. (2018). *Kulini*: Framing ethical listening and power-sensitive dialogue in remote Aboriginal education and research. *Decolonising Research Practices, 22*, pp. 26–37.

Pigza, J. (2016). The POWER model: Five core elements for teaching community-based research. In M. Beckhman and J.F Long. (Eds.), *Community-based research: Teaching for impact*, pp. 93–107. Sterling, VA: Stylus.

Rawsthorne, M. & de Pree, A. (2019). Are we welcome here? Building trust through community-based research. In A. Kover & G. Franger (Eds.), *University and society: Interdependencies and exchange*, pp. 140–157. Cheltenham, UK: Edward Elgar Press.

Rigney, L. (1999). Internationalization of an Indigenous anticolonial cultural critique of research methodologies: A guide to Indigenist research methodology and its principles. *Wicazo Sa Review, 14*(2), pp. 109–121.

Russell-Mundine, G. (2012). Reflexivity in Indigenous research: Reframing and decolonising research? *Journal of Hospitality and Tourism Management, 19*, pp. 85–90.

Shay, M. (2019). Extending the yarning yarn: Collaborative yarning methodology for ethical Indigenist education research. *The Australian Journal of Indigenous Education*, pp. 1–9. doi: doi:10.1017/jie.2018.25

Simon, R. I. (2011). A shock to thought: Curatorial judgment and the public exhibition of 'difficult knowledge.' *Memory Studies, 4*(4), pp. 432–449.

Smith, L. T. (1999). *Decolonizing methodologies: Research and Indigenous peoples.* London: Zed Books.

Soriede, G. E. (2006). Narrative construction of teacher identity: Positioning and negotiation. *Teachers and Teaching Theory and Practice, 12*, pp. 527–547.

Terarre, M. & Rawsthorne, M. (2019). Country is yarning to me: Worldview, health and well-being amongst Australian First Nations people. *British Journal of Social Work, 50*(3), pp. 1–17.

Tuhawai Smith, L. (2012). *Decolonizing methodologies: Research and Indigenous peoples* (2nd ed.). London: Zed Books.

Walker, M., Fredericks, B., Mills, K. & Anderson, D. (2014). 'Yarning' as a method for community-based health research with Indigenous women. *The Indigenous Women's Wellness Research Program, Health Care for Women International, 35*(10), pp. 1216–1226.

Wallerstein, N. (1992). Powerlessness, empowerment and health: Implementation for health promotion programs. *American Journal of Health Promotion, 6*(3), pp. 197–205.

Wenger, E. (2000). Communities of practice and social learning systems. *Organization, 7*(2), pp. 225–246.

Wright, M., Lin, A. & O'Connell, M. (2016). Humility, inquisitiveness, and openness: Key attributes for meaningful engagement with Nyoongar people. *Advances in Mental Health, 14*(2), pp. 82–95.

9
Pushing back on 'risk': Co-designing research on self-harm and suicide with queer young people

Victoria Rawlings and Elizabeth McDermott

Public health research has, like many disciplinary fields, had a complicated and dynamic relationship with the idea of Community -Led Research (CLR). As a field that has emerged largely from medical and scientific models, much research in this area has historically constructed and treated what we now call research 'participants' as subjects. However, public health is notable in its departure from these problematic constitutions in its often-interdisciplinary machinations. Research in the area has variously incorporated understandings from medicine and science of course, but also from sociology, anthropology, human geography and other social sciences. As such, public health research represents a continually changing discipline that seeks to recognise and include the importance of emotions, motivations and impacts of humans on health actions, outcomes and experiences.

From this disciplinary complexity it becomes clear that CLR may be present in some studies and absent from others, as well as representing a range of different iterations on that continuum. Research that is understood as involving community consultation has been

V. Rawlings & E. McDermott (2021). Pushing back on 'risk': Co-designing research on self-harm and suicide with queer young people. In V. Rawlings, J. Flexner & L. Riley (Eds.), *Community-Led Research: Walking new pathways together*. Sydney: Sydney University Press.

variously labelled in this field as Community-Based Participatory Research (CBPR), Patient and Public Involvement (PPI) and others. These various approaches represent a contemporary emphasis on meaningfully involving individuals from research target communities in each step of the research process – from defining the research topic to disseminating the results (Minkler & Wallerstein, 2008). Over the past ten years, this inclusion of community members in research methodologies has become particularly popular in research that focuses on underserved and minority population groups. Jacquez and colleagues suggest that CLR is particularly relevant to these groups as they produce culturally relevant, connected knowledge that is more readily translated into action and change rather than knowledge from academic theory or outsiders. Without the voices of these communities, research can miss the contextual input necessary to represent the unique experiences of those within. In addition, community group members that are able to take part in the process are more likely to feel a sense of empowerment as they are able to exert control over an aspect that affects their lives (Minkler & Wallerstein, 2008).

One such minority group that has traditionally been excluded from this process and its benefits is children and young people (Langhout & Thomas, 2010). While these groups are often constructed as different, they ultimately experience similar construction in research processes if they are aged under 18 years (Groundwater-Smith, Dockett & Bottrel, 2015). Their exclusion from research is often 'on the basis of inferiority, dependence and vulnerability' (Velardo & Drummond, 2017, p. 7), including researchers assuming their cognitive capacities to be inadequate to understand research procedures (Jacquez et al. 2013). When this category of children or young people is combined with 'sensitive topics', this exclusion is exacerbated by structural barriers that emerge from constructions of young people as inherently 'innocent' (Robinson, 2008) and therefore requiring protection from various configurations of meaning. Through constructing children's dialogue in research as 'risky' and therefore mandating additional and specific regulation, the ease of involving them in research is reduced and, as such, they are more often excluded from the research design and collaboration phases. This comes at great cost for children and young people, as their research citizenship and voice are revoked, despite the noted and international right of children to be listened to and have their views respected (United Nations Office of the High Commissioner for Human Rights, 1990). Researchers and decision-makers should therefore listen and give due weight to the voices of children on matters that affect them (Arunkumar et al., 2018), and be cognisant of the ways that young people are immersed within their local neighbourhoods and communities on a daily basis. Children and young people deserve to be engaged in the planning processes, considering that they may be particularly vulnerable to place-specific effects on health in a variety of ways (Bogar et al., 2018). However, human research ethics committees make judgements, usually without any consultation with young people, about what is appropriate to ask children and young people about and engage them with – judgements that are often related to their age and connected hegemonic social and cultural constructions of 'risk'. This is particularly the case in research that investigates 'sensitive' topics – especially those that complicate traditional constructions of children and young people as being innocent and in need of protection.

One of these intersections of meaning is in relation to sexuality and gender identity. As is seen in various policies, the social construction of 'childhood innocence', 'operates to maintain adult-child binary power relationships and the heteronormative status quo' (Robinson & Davies, 2008, p. 223). This is of course exceptionally problematic in research that is concerned with young people and their experiences of being marginalised through their lived gender identity or sexuality. As such, there is a notable dearth of research that investigates how this kind of research might meaningfully engage with young people in co-creating research initiatives in this area. Instead, it is likely that a multitude of researchers in this area face barriers to commencing such initiatives, as those that have faced diminished rights and resources in their communities – such as minority gender and sexuality youth – are more difficult to access through common research protocols, let alone CLR designs (Groundwater-Smith, et al., 2015).

Another element that is constructed as threatening childhood innocence, though less researched than panics around gender and sexuality, is that of self-harm and suicide. This is again linked to dominant constructions of young people as being at risk of 'sensitive' discussions, even if they self-identify as part of the community in question. Lakeman and Fitzgerald's (2009b) international survey of ethics committee members found that 65 per cent expressed concerns that suicidal behaviours or feelings may be increased by participating in research on the matter. Researchers in this field often share these concerns, and consequently often put in place protocols such as clinical training in risk assessment, the monitoring of participant wellbeing during data collection, detailed warnings of potential distress within patient information sheets and debriefing and follow-up care (Biddle, et al., 2013). However, other research indicates that participation in research on this topic can be beneficial or therapeutic, rather than distressing. There are few studies that report on participant distress due to participation. This suggests that ethics committees can be paternalistic and 'overprotective' and lack an understanding of the perspectives and processes of the people involved (Biddle, et al., 2013; Lakeman & Fitzgerald, 2009a).

The project that we report on here is one that dealt with a confluence of these two 'risky' elements of research, investigating the intersection between youth, sexuality/gender identity and self-harm and suicide (for further details on this project, see McDermott, Hughes & Rawlings, 2018a; McDermott, Hughes & Rawlings, 2018b). Clearly, the combinations of meanings and constructions of discussions with youth as 'risky' in relation to sexuality, gender identity and self-harm and suicide, make not only community involvement and consultation, but CLR particularly difficult. Perhaps as an outcome of this, former research of youth involvement in research of this nature is scarce; however, broader research, such as that within this book, does clearly indicate that community involvement can meaningfully impact research conceptualisation, design, recruitment, dissemination and community satisfaction and relationships with researchers.

In light of this, we grappled with ways to meaningfully (rather than tokenistically) involve young people in the process of research with the knowledge that this involvement would benefit every stage of the research. We recognised the extensive benefits of this process not only to the research, but also to the young people, including possible increases in their awareness of their own democratic rights as citizens; positive impacts on the attachment to their local environments (Checkoway & Richards-Schuster, 2003; Matthews & Limb, 2010);

opportunities for 'mutual learning' between young people and members of diverse communities; and the co-creation of healthier spaces and more liveable urban environments for people of all ages (Hohenemser & Marshall, 2002; O'Connor, 2013). These are only a few of the detailed benefits for youth in being involved in the formulation of research projects (for an extensive report on these benefits, see Arunkumar, et al., 2018; Jacquez, et al., 2013). This chapter reflects on some of the challenges that we faced in this process, but also reports on the processes, intentions and benefits that we enacted and encountered throughout. Through sharing some of the conceptual and logistical efforts that were expended by us as researchers, and by community members as expert consultants, in this chapter we hope to cast some light on how future initiatives in this field could collaborate with community members in practical ways.

The project and community involvement

The limited evidence-base of projects around youth, sexuality, gender identity and self-harm and suicide makes it exceptionally difficult to develop suicide prevention policy, deliver appropriate and effective mental health services, and tailor interventions to prevent suicide for this particular group. In this project we recognised that the need for these outcomes could only be fulfilled with a community-informed – if not distinctly community-led – approach. The distinction between those two terms is important, and this chapter, nor the project that emerged, does not make a claim to suggest that it was community-led in its entirety. If it had been, the nexus of youth, sexuality, gender identity, self-harm and suicidality would have been an exceptionally prohibiting factor to receiving funding and ethical approval within current frameworks that operate in the health research field (Lakeman & Fitzgerald, 2009b). In light of these difficulties, this project took the approach that while the community may not have a distinct hand in designing the research questions or methodology, they could be actively involved in each stage of the research including the design of data collection questions, recruitment of participants, data analysis, the writing up of the research report and the dissemination of results to communities.

In light of these considerations, from its conception our research included plans to involve the community in two ways. First, to have a research management group to steer the project in a collaborative way, and include a community consultant as part of this group to contribute to every aspect of the project. This was enacted as a paid position, reflecting our beliefs that community consultants are experts, and our commitment to treat them as such. The community member was consulted at all stages of the conception, application, procedure and reporting of the research, and was a crucial consultant for determining various directions and actions of the project. Crucially, this person was a young LGBTIQ+ person who had experience of self-harming and suicidal ideation, with strong links to the LGBTIQ+ community. They often proceeded to consult with others in this community between meetings, producing an effective and collective consultation.

Second, once ethics for the project was approved, we partnered with a local LGBTQ+ youth group in the North West of England to create a Youth Advisory Group (YAG). The group would consist of young people who were in the target age range (under 25 years of age), were sexuality or gender diverse and had experienced self-harm or suicidal ideation. The group sent out an invitation to those they thought would be eligible and interested in participating via email, and asked them to express if they were interested in consulting the researchers. Seven people volunteered and formed the YAG, convened in an initial meeting on site at the youth group with one of the researchers. In this initial meeting we discussed the potential benefits and risks for participating in the YAG, the rationale for having a YAG, collaboratively negotiated general expectations of YAG members in terms of contributions, and explored the major themes and objectives of the research project. From there, the young people proposed that a closed (private) Facebook group was the best way of staying in contact, and this was subsequently created by one of the young people. The researchers contacted the YAG using this Facebook group to ask for comments or feedback on various aspects of the research process. Some YAG members were more active on this group than others, and involvement ebbed and flowed for each individual over time; however, the researchers would always receive at least one response to their enquiries. This method enabled members of the YAG to fluidly adjust their level of participation, depending on various factors, such as their comfort level, mental health, time commitments and interests or experiences – a crucial component in establishing positive youth-specific research consultancies (Arunkumar et al., 2018; Ergler, 2017). There were also three face-to-face meetings with the group over the course of the project.

Jacquez and colleagues (2013) suggest that academic investigators might be reluctant to partner with young people due to a concern that they will not be able to understand empirical concepts or have adequate cognitive skills. However, they argue that children and young people have the 'cognitive capacity to understand basic research concepts when the material is presented in a contextually appropriate way' (Jacquez, et al., 2013, p. 177). As such, there is a requirement for research teams to actively plan and provide structure and training for any youth partners to create a research pedagogy for the project. In all meetings and interactions online, the young people in the advisory group were given opportunities to ask questions, explain hesitations and contribute their expert knowledge. The successful establishment of an environment where these interactions were possible was in part due to the facilitation of the group, undertaken by one of the researchers who was also an experienced youth educator.

Youth expertise and contributions to the YAG were acknowledged in a number of ways. First, the partnering LGBTIQ+ youth group that arranged consultation with their members, as well as a site for meetings, were paid a consultancy/collaboration fee. This fee allowed the organisation to continue with and extend their vital work with the community – work that many participants indicated was crucial to their mental, social and overall wellbeing. In addition, YAG members were provided with consultancy fees to reflect acknowledgement of their expertise and value to the project. Finally, some members of the YAG requested (and were provided with) references for jobs and other positions that spoke to their positions as advisory group members on a major national research project. In each of these initiatives we attempted to ensure that the YAG members were empowered and felt valued in their contributions. While we did not collect individual reflections on the experiences of the young people in the YAG, the majority of the members provided active contributions over the two-year period of the research project, and these contributions added to the overwhelming success of the research project.

In this chapter, we focus specifically on how the YAG contributed to the second of two stages of this mixed method research. The first stage involved undertaking 30 qualitative interviews (15 online, 15 face-to-face) to establish a deep understanding of the participants' experiences. The second stage utilised the garnered data to develop an online questionnaire that was eventually completed by almost 1000 participants around England. In both stages the YAG was a crucial mediator of research procedures, and their interventions meaningfully altered the processes of the research; however, this was particularly the case in the design of the youth survey. While semi-structured interview questions were changed slightly due to consultation with the YAG, the survey underwent more extensive changes to language choices and response options.

Developing a youth survey: meaningful consultations with the Youth Advisory Group

Consultation with members of the YAG was convened to pilot and provide feedback on the online questionnaire (youth survey) prior to its release. This was achieved through conducting individual and group interviews both online and in person with four group members after a final draft of the youth survey was completed. Specifically, we asked the members to 'talk out loud' their thought processes as they interpreted and answered the survey questions. This assisted us to identify linguistic, cultural, structural and logical problems with the various questions (Addington-Hall, 2007).

Those in the YAG were asked if they would like to contribute to the development of the survey. Each participant was informed about the nature of the study as well as which stage the project was at, clarifying the aims of the interview. They were each asked to 'think aloud' as they completed the survey as they would in any other context. This process required each volunteer to read the question aloud, and then continue to speak about what they thought it meant and any problems that they had encountered when deciding how to answer. Prior to commencing, the researcher who had previously worked with the YAG and was therefore known to them demonstrated what this looked like and encouraged participants to also think/talk about their comprehension of the question, the response options that were present, the language, look, feel and length of the survey and the effort involved in responding. The researcher also asked probing, spontaneous questions to the participants throughout this process that related to verbal and non-verbal cues of the participant such as hesitations, confusion or uncertainty (Murtagh, Addington-Hall & Higginson, 2007). This process provided significant and valuable feedback for the survey.

Two of the young people from the YAG wished to take part in this process but were unable to meet face-to-face for various reasons. At their request, we organised to send them the survey within the software as it would be seen by future participants. We asked them again to make comments on the question inclusion, wording and language used, as well as the responses and whether they felt anything could be improved. We also asked for comments from them around the look and feel of the survey as well as its length. Although this was not necessarily in the 'read aloud' format, it gave us insight into what it might look for young people to complete the survey in 'real time' without a researcher in the room with them. In this way, we established two environments for the pre-testing of the survey including four pilot testers: Lucy (18, cisgender woman, lesbian, White British), Dylan (17, transgender man, unsure, White British), Anthony (18, transgender man, straight, White British) and Rebecca (18, cisgender woman, bisexual, White British).

As our research approach sought to prioritise subjugated knowledge and marginalised voices, the perspective of these volunteers was of critical concern. Their feedback was both positive and negative; they reflected that they felt motivated to complete the survey, that they liked the design and functionality of the survey, and that the vast majority of responses for multiple choice questions matched their experiences with self-harm, suicidal feelings and help seeking. This affirmed many of the choices that we made around what options to include, especially after our adaptations from previous studies of self-harm and suicidal reasons (Hawton, Rodham & Evans, 2006).

Consulting with young people enabled us to understand survey items where young people may be more likely to drop out of the survey due to incomprehension or a lack of suitable responses.

After receiving the feedback of the volunteers, the research team reviewed the items highlighted in interviews and examined the potential for alterations. In particular, we focused on items that could potentially lead to response error, either through difficulties with comprehension or a lack of applicable answers for participants to select, making them feel corralled into particular responses that may not apply to them.

These interviews led to changes in 14 questions in the survey which had, in total, 49 response items. The changes related to the provision of relevant answer options, the language used, the structure/ procedure of questions and some of the information given in blurb/introduction sections. Crucially, the young people altered questions about gender identity and sexuality – survey questions that are notoriously difficult to design (McDermott & Rawlings, 2015), particularly amongst young people who are less likely to ascribe to traditionally accepted/endorsed labels (McDermott, et al., 2013). While the researchers had gathered 'best practice' information on how to ask about gender identity, and done extensive research on how questions had been previously asked in similar studies, this did not match with the preferences of the YAG volunteers. For example, a question that asked explicitly 'what is your gender identity' initially included four options – and with the feedback of Anthony, it was changed to have five. See below for the original and amended question.

Original item	Amended item
2A. What is your gender identity?	2A. What is your gender identity?
<ul><li>Male</li><li>Female</li><li>Non-binary</li><li>Other – please specify_____</li></ul>	<ul><li>Male</li><li>Female</li><li>Non-binary</li><li>Gender fluid</li><li>Other – please specify_____</li></ul>

In commenting on the need for this change, Anthony contributed:

there is no option of 'both' [or] 'gender fluid' which could be covered under the 'other' option but it kind of seems as though they aren't taken as seriously as male, female or non binary people. That however is me just being picky and isn't an urgent change but if it wasn't too much hassle it may be an option? Just so everyone is happy?

The research team discussed this feedback and recognised that including particular categories does lead to a hierarchy of gender identity categories. We considered including, as Anthony suggested, both 'gender fluid' and 'both'; however, we felt that non-binary and 'other' provided enough options for those who might wish to identify as both male and female in a static way. However, we did feel that it was likely that many participants may identify as gender fluid, and to include this option would demonstrate a greater understanding from the project.

Another gender identity question was also impacted by this process. This item was utilised to establish whether participants were trans or had diverse gender identities.

Original item	Amended item
2B. What was your sex at birth? • Male • Female • Intersex • Other – please specify_____	2B. Do you identify with the sex assigned to you at birth? • Yes • No • Unsure

Dylan, who identified as transgender, suggested that the question could cause trans participants distress when they were asked to identify with their birth sex. Although we initially followed guidelines for this question from Mitchell and Howarth (2009), his contributions highlighted that young participants may have different experiences of this question being asked. Those in the YAG understood sex and gender as less fixed, more fluid and more nuanced than the (older) literature suggested. This was particularly the case for questions around sexual orientation and gender identity, where the participants provided significant and helpful input. The research team agreed that there was no direct need to ask this question in its original format; rather, the emendation achieved the same result (identifying trans or non-binary participants) without causing any distress or burden for the participant.

Issues were also noted about questions that related to sexual attractions. In the below item, volunteers identified problems with the fixity of biologically determined and binary, dichotomous categories of 'sex'.

Original item	Amended item
4A. Which one of these statements best describes your sexual attractions at the moment?	4A. Which one of these statements best describes your sexual attractions at the moment?
• I am attracted only to people of my own sex • I am attracted to people of all sexes • I am attracted only to people of the opposite sex • I am not sure to whom I am attracted	• I am mostly attracted to people of my own gender • I am attracted to people of all genders • I am mostly attracted to people of the opposite gender • I am not sure to whom I am attracted

Lucy reflected that although she identified as a lesbian, she had a trans girlfriend, and this question confused her as it asked her to identify the sex (biologically determined) that she is attracted to. Dylan encountered difficulties answering this question because he was still unsure about his attractions, but was also confronted by the use of 'sex' for the same reasons as Lucy. Dylan suggested the addition of 'gender' and changing from 'only' to 'mostly' to enable broader selection categories. Anthony, in his online contribution, wrote:

> when it asks who you are attracted to, it says sex, for me, I'm attracted to people of the opposite gender. I feel that this is totally different from people of the opposite sex. By saying people of the

opposite sex it suggests I like males. Which isn't correct. But by saying people of the same sex it makes me feel as though the people behind the survey view me as female, also, that disregards transwomen who by their sex, ie their chromosomes would technically have the sex male. I feel that that question in particular needs to be changed in some way as a priority.

Again, this captures the complexity and fluidity of young people's lived realities, their rejection of what many construct as simple or straightforward questions, and the incongruence of former measures to their lives – all aspects that might not have been captured without this consultation process. This question was initially adapted from Hillier and colleagues' (2010) ground-breaking study of young same-sex attracted people; however, the emendations to the question, drawn from young people's accounts, make it potentially more valid for participants in this study. Responses were initially amended to include sex/gender, which Anthony rejected through explaining:

I think gender is the best option and sack sex off as if you have both it then gets more confusing! Because I'm attracted to people of the opposite gender to me but they are the same sex as me, if that makes sense?

As such, we altered the response further to include 'gender' only, and 'mostly' to enable recognition of fluidity and non-binary identifications.

Other questions that the young people requested alterations to were around religion, social class, experiences of abuse, hiding of sexuality and/or gender identity, reasons for not seeking help, people that participants might seek help from and the level of helpfulness from these sources. Some of these ended up being crucial changes in terms of final response rates. For example, one item (below) asked about participants' non-disclosure of their sexuality and/or gender identity during periods of time when they were self-harming or experiencing suicidal feelings.

Original item	Amended item
11D. Thinking about times when you have self-harmed/had suicidal feelings, why did you not tell some people about your sexual orientation/gender identity? (tick up to four options)	11D. Thinking about periods of time when you have self-harmed/had suicidal feelings, why did you not tell some people about your sexual orientation/gender identity? (select all that apply)
• I told everyone I needed to • It was not necessary • I was pretending to be straight/cisgender • I did not want to be treated differently • I thought that they would reject me • I was afraid • I felt ashamed • I felt abnormal • I had seen others badly treated after coming out • I thought my family would be disappointed • It was private • I did not think they would believe me • Other (please specify)_____	• I told everyone I needed to • It was not necessary • I was pretending to be straight/cisgender • I did not want to be treated differently • I thought that they would reject me • I was afraid • I felt ashamed • I felt abnormal • I had seen others badly treated after coming out • I thought my family would be disappointed • It was private • I did not think they would believe me • Other (please specify)_____

First, Dylan suggested that he did not know to what time period this was referring – if it was related specifically to moments of self-harm or suicidal moments, or to general time periods where self-harm and suicidal feelings were occurring. Wording was altered to try to express more clearly that the question sought to know about periods of time rather than self-harm and suicidal moments. In addition, this question, or rather the required response format, was highlighted as problematic by Anthony. Specifically, he contended that the 'choose up to four options' format was difficult for him to fulfil as he identified that there were six options that he wanted to choose but couldn't. Lucy and Dylan also had issues with only selecting four responses for this question. As such, the research team resolved to relinquish this restriction and allow participants to select as many options as were relevant to them.

The reason that this constraint was initially included, and remains on some other items, was to ensure that data produced was valid, and that participants did not necessarily choose 'easily' but were compelled to choose their responses carefully. Anthony, however, demonstrated that this restriction was not necessarily causing him to think more about his answers:

> I went with the top four as I pressed them first and couldn't be bothered changing them that's why I think more than four may be good as then you will be able to fully understand what people are feeling, whereas if you leave it at four you may find the lower ones get ignored.

This question and the others where 'select four' is the instruction had 'randomisation' of answers, ensuring that the 'top four' options (and indeed the rest) were always in a different order/format. Randomisation was chosen to ensure validity of responses; however, enabling participants in this question to 'select all' was adopted as an amendment due to the YAG consultation.

In terms of results, this was a crucial change. Of the 752 participants that eventually responded to the question, they indicated 3455 data points, equating to an average of 4.6 selections per participant. Some participants indicated that many more than four options were relevant to them, indicating the complexity of young people's lives and decisions about disclosure. This change, however, did not result in a majority of young people choosing all of the options. What it did produce was a freedom for participants, and consequently a more reliable and reflective dataset.

Survey outcomes: impacts of the Youth Advisory Group

Working with an exceptionally marginalised group meant that establishing a large sample size for the survey would always be a difficult task. Part of the rationale for including and working closely with the YAG, including in their expertise for question design, was to enable the questionnaire/survey to be accessible, understandable and comfortable for participants to complete, thus reducing the typical 'drop out' of participants that naturally occurs during survey participation. From the 835 eligible participants that commenced the survey, only 46 did not complete the final item, meaning that there was a drop-out rate of only 5.5 percent. The quantity of participants in this stage was also a crucial component of this research and while it was determined that a statistically powerful sample size would be 400 participants, the final number of eligible participants 'counted' in the data was 789 young people. While we have no direct evidence that the YAG assisted with both of these outcomes, it is clear that the overwhelming majority of participants were motivated, felt represented and that they were able to answer each item comfortably. In terms of recruitment, the YAG again assisted in publicising the research in their online and offline social networks. Although we cannot provide statistics on how participants came to take part in the research, it seemed that personal knowledge of the project and investment in an invitation yielded more participants than a general 'mention' of the project. Exposure of the survey to great numbers was not everything – it was also the type of exposure and where this came from, as well as the experience of taking the survey – an experience that was positively impacted by the survey's construction and inclusive practices. Some of this can be illustrated in the final survey item, where participants were given an opportunity to openly answer the question 'Is there anything else that you want to tell us?'. Some participants took the time to reflect on their positive experiences undertaking the questionnaire, for example:

> I thought this questionnaire was really well done.
> This survey was really good, and i love the diversity and the terms used instead of asking 'are you male or female?' you have more diverse options and instead of asking 'are you gay or straight?' you gave much more diverse options which is amazing so thank you for making me feel included
> This is a cool survey, you are first people I have come out. It's progress and it's making me feel better
> I found this survey very interesting and actually gained some insight into myself through answering the questions – thank you.

I actually think this survey was helpful to me in thinking about why I did self harm and what I was thinking at the time.

These comments speak strongly to the resistance of many around discussing 'sensitive topics' like sexuality, gender identity and self-harm and suicide with young people. Throughout the research project, our experience indicated that the young people benefited from talking about their experiences, feelings and thoughts, and had rarely been given such an opportunity to do so before. That a survey could make someone 'feel better', or 'be helpful to me', or make 'me feel included', or produce 'insight into myself', is a compelling reason for future research with, by and for young people experiencing distress.

Some participants also provided further suggestions for improvement in questions on sexuality and gender identity:

Suggestions: add questions about romantic attraction as well as sexual attraction, give option to say you feel no sexual attraction at all (i.e. you're asexual), separate questions about coming out as not-straight & coming as trans, & the subsequent reactions/effects – people can be out as one but not the other, can get negative reactions about one but not the other, etc.

Regarding the question of who I am attracted to, I found those four options somewhat limiting, and although there was a return to sexual orientation shortly after, I probably would have preferred an 'Other' option, as some identities wouldn't really fit neatly into the four options given. Overall I think this is an important line of research, and I am glad you are out there doing the work.

Please put 'no sexual attraction' as an option. Surely it's deeply unhelpful to deny respondents the ability to self identify in a form about suicide and self harm.

These comments further illustrate the power and potential of meaningful, extensive and ongoing consultations with members of the community who are directly affected by research processes and outcomes. If we were to rewrite and re-administer the survey, these voices would be listened to, and these questions altered. As it is, these contributions have impacted our research projects and approaches since.

Conclusion

While the above may read as a simple piloting process, we argue that the community involvement of this process was both transformative to the research, and that this stage of the research would not have been successful without the connected work that was done with, by and for the community within our research design. The interviews with YAG volunteers formed just one component of this project, and were facilitated by four key factors. These included a long-term building of relationships between the researcher and the group; consistent recognition of the expertise and importance of the individuals involved, including remuneration for time and energy expended; a similar relationship built with their LGBTIQ+ youth group and its leadership; and ongoing conversations about all other elements of the research process and design.

Although we have reported here on only one (vital) element of how the YAG impacted on the data collection of the Queer Futures project, they had extensive other contributions throughout the two-year duration. This included informing recruitment strategies, advising how we could best get in contact with a dispersed, intersectional, sometimes disconnected, often distressed population; assisting with recruitment by sharing the research in their own networks; influencing interview questions language, order and structure in the first stage of the research; consulting on the design of the project website and name; consulting on the final report for youth and community; sharing the research report in their networks (disseminating results); and attending and contributing to the concluding symposium for the research which was a 'coming together' of the researchers, stakeholders and community groups.

Without those affected by the research question on board, it was unlikely that the research would be well taken up by the community, produce a positive experience for participants or achieve a breadth in communicating the results. Our approach with the YAG was to meaningfully include young people's voices along the way in terms of project design (research questions, interview questions, procedures and survey measures) to make sure that the project was best serving the target group. In addition, YAG advice made it possible to improve recruitment, dissemination of results and the overall participant experience.

It is important to recognise that in the final report of the Queer Futures study, this extensive theoretical and practical work was only referenced in a short paragraph that detailed the presence of the YAG. While the report necessarily reduces the complexities of the study down to a more brief, digestible document, this section was particularly reduced. As such, we felt it necessary to contribute a more detailed and in-depth reflection on the importance of the community's involvement in this project. While potentially this iteration of CLR was not as consistent or comprehensive as others that have occurred, the involvement of and consultation with LGBTIQ+ young people who had self-harmed or attempted suicide as an advisory group was crucial to its success. These contributions increased the comfort of research participants, improved the quality of research measures, and enabled a more diverse communication of research results. In addition, their inputs and investments into the project resulted in greater sharing within their networks, improving recruitment to the study. Each of these considerations is invaluable in a study that seeks to include a marginalised and hard-to-reach population that is often distrustful of research but actively seeking to make a positive contribution to their situation and community. In other words, the involvement of community members in this research was critical to its success, but also beneficial to participants in a multitude of ways. Our experience further demonstrates the argument that despite the difficulty of conceptualising possibilities for community involvement in 'sensitive' research, the efforts produce significant impacts throughout the research process. CLR in public health, and more specifically in research that includes minority, disadvantaged and at-risk populations, is crucial if research is to ultimately benefit the population that is included.

Acknowledgements

The authors would like to thank all of the participants in the Queer Futures project, especially the community groups and individuals within the LGBTIQ+ community who shared their time, expertise and connections with the study.

References

Addington-Hall, J. M. (2007). Survey research: Methods of data collection, questionnaire design and piloting. In J. M. Addington-Hall, E. Bruera, I. J. Higginson, & S. Payne (Eds.), *Research methods in palliative care*, pp. 61–81. Oxford: Oxford University Press.

Arunkumar, K., Bowman, D. D., Coen, S. E., El-Bagdady, M. A., Ergler, C. R., Gilliland, J. A., ... Paul, S. (2018). Conceptualizing youth participation in children's health research: Insights from a youth-driven process for developing a youth advisory council. *Children, 6*(1). doi: 10.3390/children6010003

Biddle, L., Cooper, J., Owen-Smith, A., Klineberg, E., Bennewith, O., Hawton, K., ... Gunnell, D. (2013). Qualitative interviewing with vulnerable populations: Individuals' experiences of participating in suicide and self-harm based research. *Journal of Affective Disorders, 145*(3). doi:10.1016/j.jad.2012.08.024.

Bogar, S., Young, S., Woodruff, S., Beyer, K., Mitchell, R. & Johnson, S. (2018). More than gangsters and girl scouts: Environmental health perspectives of urban youth. *Health Place, 54*, pp. 50–64.

Checkoway, B. & Richards-Schuster, K. (2003). Youth participation in community evaluation research. *American Journal of Evaluation, 24*(1), pp. 21–33.

Ergler, C. (2017). Beyond passive participation: From research on to research by children. In R. Evans, Skelton, T., Holt, L. (Ed.), *Methodological approaches, Vol. 2*, pp. 97–115. Berlin: Springer.

Groundwater-Smith, S., Dockett, S. & Bottrel, D. (2015). *Participatory research with children and young people.* Los Angeles: SAGE.

Hawton, K., Rodham, K. & Evans, E. (2006). *By their own young hand: Deliberate self-harm and suicidal ideas in adolescents.* London: Jessica Kingsley Publishers.

Hillier, L., Jones, T., Monagle, M., Overton, N., Gahan, L., Blackman, J. & Mitchell, A. (2010). *Writing themselves in 3: The third national study on the sexual health and wellbeing of same-sex attracted and gender-questioning young people*. Melbourne: Australian Research Centre in Sex, Health and Society (ARCSHS), La Trobe University.

Hohenemser, L. K. & Marshall, B. D. (2002). Utilizing a youth development framework to establish and maintain a youth advisory committee. *Health Promotion Practitioner, 3*(2), pp. 155–165.

Jacquez, F., Vaughn, L. & Wagner, E. (2013). Youth as partners, participants or passive recipients: A review of children and adolescents in community-based participatory research (CBPR). *American Journal of Community Psychology, 51*(1), pp. 176–189.

Lakeman, R. & Fitzgerald, M. (2009a). Ethical suicide research: A survey of researchers. *International Journal of Mental Health Nursing, 18*(1), pp. 10–17.

Lakeman, R. & Fitzgerald, M. (2009b). The ethics of suicide research: The views of ethics committee members. *Crisis, 30*(1), pp. 13–19.

Langhout, R. D. & Thomas, E. (2010). Imagining participatory action research in collaboration with children: An introduction. *American Journal of Community Psychology, 46*(1–2), pp. 60–66. doi:10.1007/s10464-010-9321-1.

Matthews, H. & Limb, M. (2010). Another white elephant? Youth councils as democratic structures. *Space Polity, 7*(2), pp. 173–192.

McDermott, E., Hughes, E. & Rawlings, V. (2018a). Norms and normalisation: Understanding lesbian, gay, bisexual, transgender and queer youth, suicidality and help-seeking. *Culture, Health & Sexuality, 20*(2), pp. 156–172.

McDermott, E., Hughes, E. & Rawlings, V. (2018b). The social determinants of lesbian, gay, bisexual and transgender youth suicidality in England: A mixed methods study. *Journal of Public Health, 40*(3), pp. 244–251.

McDermott, E. & Rawlings, V. (2015). Online surveys. In A. E. Goldberg (Ed.), *The SAGE encyclopdia of LGBTQ studies*. London: SAGE.

Minkler, M. & Wallerstein, N. (Eds.) (2008). *Community-based participatory research in health, process to outcomes* (2nd ed.). San Francisco, CA: Jossey-Bass.

Mitchell, M. & Howarth, C. (2009). *Trans research review*. Manchester: Equity & Human Rights Commission.

Murtagh, F. E., Addington-Hall, J. M. & Higginson, I. J. (2007). The value of cognitive interviewing techniques in palliative care research. *Palliative Medicine, 21*(2), pp. 87–93.

O'Connor, C. D. (2013). Engaging young people? The experiences, challenges, and successes of Canadian youth advisory councils. In J. Taft, L. E. Bass & S. K. Nenga (Eds.), *Youth engagement: The civic-political lives of children and youth*, pp. 73–96. Bingley, UK: Emerald Books.

Robinson, K. (2008). In the name of 'childhood innocence': A discursive exploration of the moral panic associated with childhood and sexuality. *Cultural Studies Review, 14*(2), pp. 113–129.

Robinson, K., & Davies, C. (2008). Docile bodies and heteronormative moral subjects: Constructing the child and sexual knowledge in schooling. *Sexuality and Culture, 12*(4), pp. 221–239. doi:10.1007/s12119-008-9037-7.

United Nations Office of the High Commissioner for Human Rights (1990). Convention on the Rights of the Child: Adopted and opened for signature, ratification and accession by General Assembly resolution 44/25 of 20 November 1989 entry into force 2 September 1990, in accordance with article 49.

About the authors

Cathie Burgess is a non-Indigenous associate professor at the University of Sydney who has spent over 35 years working in Indigenous education in schools and universities. She is a parent of Aboriginal children and is closely connected to the Redfern community through family, work and sports. Cathie's work centres local Aboriginal community voices in her teaching and research programs. She coordinates undergraduate and postgraduate Aboriginal Studies, Learning from Country and Leadership in Aboriginal Education programs. As Aboriginal Studies Association NSW President, Cathie maintains strong connections with schools across the state as well as advocating for Aboriginal Studies through government submissions, speaking engagements and convening annual conferences for teachers, Aboriginal community consultants and students. Her current research includes the Culturally Nourishing Schooling Project, Learning from Country in the City, the Smith Family Learning from Life Scholarship Program and Aboriginal Middle Leaders in NSW Schools.

Sheelagh Daniels-Mayes is an Indigenous Australian Kamilaroi woman who lost her eyesight as a child following measles. Sheelagh is located with the Indigenous Research Hub and is the coordinator for the Sydney Indigenous Research Network. Her work focuses on Aboriginal education, Indigenous Studies and methodologies, and she is a disability scholar and activist. Sheelagh is particularly concerned with higher education's responsibilities in achieving equity and social justice for society's marginalised people. She uses Critical Race Theory, cultural responsiveness and Critical Access Studies alongside Indigenous methodologies.

James Flexner is senior lecturer in historical archaeology and heritage at the University of Sydney. His interests include historical archaeology, landscape archaeology, the Oceanic region, and how to build a better world for human beings to live in. James has done extensive fieldwork in the Pacific Islands and Australia, currently focusing on projects in Vanuatu and collaborative research with Australian South Sea Islanders in tropical Queensland.

Allan Hall is a proud descendant of the Gamilaroi and Yuwaallaraay people. In his 30 years working with the NSW Department of Education he has worked as a classroom teacher, principal, Aboriginal education consultant and he is currently a Senior Aboriginal Education and Engagement Advisor at the Bangamalanha Centre. Allan has worked alongside researchers such as Dr Tyson Yunkaporta in the past and has been instrumental in the design and delivery of 8 Ways pedagogy.

Yvonne Hill is a proud Wiradjuri woman who works for the NSW Department of Education as an Aboriginal education and engagement officer at the Bangamalanha Centre. She has been a classroom teacher and assistant principal in numerous schools over her career and is recognised as a passionate educator and advocate for community. Yvonne has contributed to improving research practice by guiding and working with many researchers over the past 20 years.

Amanda Howard's work and research are focused on work with communities in all its forms. She is interested in the way people self-organise and enact networked and relational leadership in a variety of different contexts. From disaster planning and recovery to community action groups, disability inclusion and informal neighbourhood connections, the ways in which people navigate complexity to get things done is endlessly interesting and will occupy her for a long while to come. She has written across these areas including *Everyday community practice* (2019) and *Working with communities: Critical perspectives* (2011) with Margot Rawsthorne. Amanda works in Social Work and Policy Studies at the University of Sydney.

Meaghan Katrak is a social worker with over 30 years' experience working alongside communities. Meaghan's work experience within Indigenous and mainstream contexts encompasses community development, program planning, delivery and evaluation, direct social work practice, research and academia. Meaghan lives and works in Sydney but calls the Mallee home.

Elizabeth McDermott is a professor of health inequality at Lancaster University. Her research considers mental health inequality, especially in relation to age, sexuality, gender and social class. She has conducted studies investigating suicide, self-harm, emotional distress, wellbeing and happiness. Her research attempts to investigate and develop understandings of the social, economic and cultural origins of mental health and wellbeing, and produce evidence which can inform policy and practice.

Anthony McKnight is an Awabakal, Gumaroi and Yuin man. Anthony is a father, husband, uncle, son, grandson, brother, cousin, nephew, friend and cultural man. Anthony is currently a senior lecturer in the School of Education, Faculty of the Arts, Social Sciences and Humanities at the University of Wollongong. Anthony respects Country and values the knowledge that has been taught to him from Country, Elders and teachers from community(s). He continuously and respectfully incorporates Aboriginal ways of knowing and learning, with a particular interest in contributing to placing Country centre to validate Aboriginal approaches in academia and schools. Anthony in 2017 completed a PhD called *Singing up Country in academia: Teacher education academics and preservice teachers' experience with Yuin Country*. He holds a Masters of Education (HRD) from the University of Sydney and a Bachelor of Education, Health and Physical Education from the University of Wollongong.

Samantha McMahon's research interests include sociology of education, inclusive education and widening university participation. Her work explores how teachers' engagement with multiple knowledges affects the equity of student experience and how students' lived experiences impact their understandings of education. Sam's mainly ethnographic research includes participation in the AIME Research Partnership (the Australian Indigenous Mentoring Experience), widening participation programs and NSW public schools. Her two current research projects include evaluations of widening participation programs for students experiencing socioeconomic disadvantage, and shifting discourses of gap year and university for regional students in NSW (e.g. https://astar.tv/gapyear/). Sam works at the University of Sydney in initial teacher education, teaching units of study in sociology of education, professional research projects and pedagogical approaches in education.

Imelda Miller is a curator at the Queensland Museum responsible for the Torres Strait Islander and Pacific Islander collections. Imelda works with material culture and archival collections inside and outside of the traditional museum environment to create access to collections for communities of origin. Imelda's Australian South Sea Islander heritage drives her passion in creating awareness about Australian South Sea Islander history, heritage and identity.

Victoria Rawlings' research focuses on the intersections between gender, sexuality, youth and social structures. Her PhD investigated the connections between gender, social structures and 'bullying' in two high schools in NSW. Following this work, Vic worked as a Senior Research Associate at Lancaster University (UK) for two years, conducting a national study on LGBTQ young people, self-harm and suicide. in 2021, Vic was awarded an Australian Research Council DECRA fellowship to conduct research in partnership with school communities around cultures of gender and sexuality. This research aims to understand how schools can positively and proactively include all students.

Margot Rawsthorne lectures in community development at the University of Sydney. Prior to joining academia she worked for 15 years in southwestern Sydney in non-government agencies. Her research focuses on the experience of inequality, particularly shaped by gender, location and sexuality. Her current projects focus on community change through community action across the fields of housing, poverty and disasters. She has a strong commitment to supporting the developing research capacity of the non-government sector and research collaboration that aims to ensure the relevance and usefulness of academic research and scholarship.

Lynette Riley, a Wiradjuri and Gamilaroi woman from Dubbo and Moree, is an associate professor in the Sydney School of Education and Social Work, University of Sydney; and program director for Indigenous Studies and Aboriginal Education. Lynette trained as an infants/primary teacher and has taught in high school; she has been an Aboriginal Education consultant for schools, an Aboriginal development manager for VET, manager of the Dubbo TAFE campuses; state manager for Aboriginal education NSW DET; and an academic at the University of New England and the University of Sydney. Her career focus has been Aboriginal Education for Aboriginal students and Indigenous studies for the wider public.

Helena Robinson is a museum studies scholar whose research explores the construction of values and significance around cultural collections. Her current projects investigate the ideas of cultural democracy and stakeholder participation in the museum. At the University of Sydney, she is a senior lecturer in interdisciplinary education with the Office of the Deputy Vice Chancellor – Education, Enterprise and Engagement.

Dara Sampson is a social worker who has worked for Centrelink in senior leadership roles then as a lecturer at the University of Newcastle. She currently teaches at the University of Sydney in Social Work and works as academic research manager for the Centre for Brain and Mental Health Research, University of Newcastle. She is passionate about the importance of people's stories and language and how language can extend or challenge social constructions, particularly as they relate to mental health and stigma. Dara is part of the research team on the Community-Led Disaster Resilience Pilot in NSW.

Cecil See is a proud Wiradjuri man who works for NSW Department of Education as an Aboriginal education and engagement officer at the Bangamalanha Centre. Cecil holds a Masters in Indigenous Language Education and is recognised for his contribution to language revival. He also has a background in health, having previously served as a chief executive officer for an Aboriginal community-controlled health service.

Emma Webster has Wendish, Prussian and English heritage and works for the University of Sydney School of Rural Health as a senior lecturer in rural research. She has a background in public health and is recognised for her pragmatic and collaborative approach to research and her genuine desire to engage academia to serve community interests.

Julie Welsh is a Gomeroi/Murawari woman. She was born on Gomeroi Country and grew up on Gadigal Country as part of the Redfern Aboriginal community from a young age. She has a Masters in Community Management and has worked for many years in community development and engagement. She is passionate about cultural strengthening and is constantly inspired by her beautiful daughters, and the incredible women and Elders around her every day in community.

Index

Index

Index

United Nations Educational, Scientific and Cultural Organization (UNESCO) 102
universities 3, 6, 25, 27, 41, 69, 96, 140, 145, 151, 158–160
University of Papua New Guinea 116
University of Queensland 89, 97
University of the Sunshine Coast 97

Vanuatu 92, 108–122
Vanuatu Kaljoral Senta (VKS) 111, 116

Watt, Agnes 116
Watt, William 116

White Australia Policy 99
whiteness 14, 147
wicked problems 49
Wilkes, Ted 150
Williams, John 114
Willie, Edson 116
Wilson, Shawn 28, 132, 133
Wiradjuri Country 74
Wollongong, New South Wales 57

yarning 78, 134, 146, 156–158
young people 55–70, 166–183
Yuin Country 57
Yunkaporta, Tyson Kaawoppa 28, 132

www.ingramcontent.com/pod-product-compliance
Lightning Source LLC
Chambersburg PA
CBHW071023280326
41935CB00011B/1462

9 781743 327579